Dedication

This book is dedicated to the obedient to go and send others to express and propagate the salvation message of Jesus Christ to all humankind throughout the world to harvest souls into the kingdom of God.

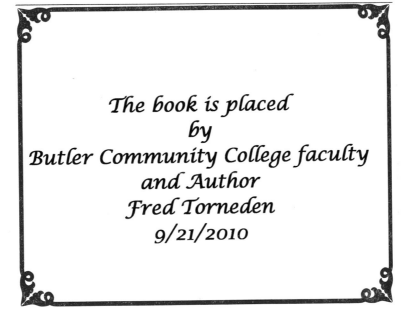

The book is placed
by
Butler Community College faculty
and Author
Fred Torneden
9/21/2010

The
Christian Expression

Fred Torneden

ISBN 978-1-58169-328-7
For Worldwide Distribution
Printed in the U.S.A.

Axiom Press
P.O. Box 191540 • Mobile, AL 36619
800-367-8203

PLEASE NOTE:
*All the proceeds in the sales of this book are designated
to ministries committed to the mandate of the Lord's
Great Commission to be witnesses unto Him to the ends of the earth
in spreading His glorious Gospel through international
evangelistic work.*

Table of Contents

CHAPTER 1

Overcome Excuses

When I was in my mid-twenties, I had some notoriety in the state of Kansas as a runner and a marathoner. I enjoyed a rewarding running career with area road race wins that culminated with the second best marathon time among United States citizens in 1984. Back in my athletic prime, some would notice my last name Torneden and ask, "Are you the runner?"

Deborah, my wife, was a state champion record holder in high school and a four-time All-American at Kansas State University. After college, she was selected to run on U.S. national teams to compete in marathons and road relays in Japan, China, and Greece. Long after I retired from racing, Deborah has continued to win local road races even into her forties. She was ranked top ten in the world for the 45-49 year age group in women's road running. A good friend of ours once told Deborah, "You're a 46-year-old who looks like a 36-year-old and runs like a 26-year-old."

When I was running at my best, I joked with some runner friends that on a national level I was the most famous marathoner that no one ever heard of. My small window of time for fleeting athletic fame is long gone now. Years after my athletic retirement, some have noticed my last name Torneden and have asked, "Are you married to the runner?" I'm waiting for the day when some young runner asks, "Did you used to be somebody? Did you used to be Fred Torneden?"

Our two boys and I enjoy being part of Deborah's three-man entourage whenever she races. I have jokingly called myself "Mr. Mom" as I took care of our two young boys while she was competing in road races. As her biggest fans, Kyle, Myles and I do our best as a family support system to help encourage Deborah to run her races to her highest potential.

Therefore we also, since we are surrounded by so great a cloud of witnesses, let us lay aside every weight, and the sin which so easily ensnares us, and let us run with endurance the race that is set before us (Heb. 12:1).

This great cloud of witnesses includes the Old Testament saints mentioned in the eleventh chapter of Hebrews who obtained a good testimony by framing their worlds with the word of God (Heb. 11:1-3). We are to be encouraged by the faith of these witnesses to persevere and finish the spiritual race set before each of us.

Extraordinary Faith

It's inspirational to consider the extraordinary faith of Noah or Abraham. These and other men and women of faith endured trials of mocking, scourging, chains, and imprisonment. They were stoned to death, sawn in two, tempted, and slain with the sword. They were destitute, afflicted, and tormented yet obtained a good testimony through faith (Heb. 11:36-39).

We can also be encouraged with the realization that these great Bible heroes of faith were clearly human just like us. We can certainly relate to the frailties and inadequacies that we all share. God used them anyway despite their mistakes and imperfectness. They each had faults to overcome.

For example, Noah had a drinking problem. Abraham was too old and lied about his wife being his sister not once, but twice. Abraham then took things (and Hagar) into his own hands to conceive Ishmael instead of waiting for Isaac in God's timing. His son Isaac was a daydreamer. His grandson Jacob was a deceptive liar.

The Hebrews 11 "Great Faith Hall of Fame" also lists Rahab, Gideon, Samson and David. Rahab was a prostitute. Gideon was afraid. Samson was a long-haired hippie who lusted after women. David murdered Bathsheba's husband to cover up their affair.

The people in the Bible all had shortcomings or circumstances to conquer. Like us, they each had an excuse for not being used by God. Joseph was abused. Jeremiah was too young. Elijah had suicidal tendencies. Jonah ran from God. Naomi was a widow. Job went bankrupt.

Our New Testament examples don't get much better. John the Baptist ate locusts. Peter denied Christ three times after he boasted to the contrary. The disciples fell asleep while praying. Martha worried about everything. Mary Magdalene was demon possessed. The Samaritan woman was divorced five times before living with a sixth man. Paul was too religious. Timothy had stomach ailments. Lazarus was dead.

In the name of political correctness, some use a process of relabeling shortcomings with nicer sounding alternatives. For example, it's considered too harsh to be called lazy. Those people are instead motivationally deficient. We're no longer ignorant—we're a knowledge-based non-possessor.

Leah, Jacob's first wife, was not less attractive than Rachel her younger sister—she was cosmetically different. Elisha wasn't bald—he was in follicle regression. Overweight Eli was merely metabolically challenged. We can call short Zacchaeus either vertically challenged or anatomically compact. Lazarus was living impaired before being raised.

Age Is No Deterrent to Accomplishment

Abraham and Noah, biblical giants of faith, were greatly used by God despite their chronological impairments. Abraham and Sarah waited 25 years before conceiving their child of promise when well-advanced in age. Noah was 500 years old when God gave him a 100-year assignment to build an ark. (God can use all of us no matter how many years young.)

Advanced age can be an excuse that becomes a detriment to effective expressions of ministry to one another. There are two gender-based facts about aging—few women admit their age and fewer men act it. It's too easy to think that God can't use the silver-haired person after their prime years because society wants to put the chronologically advanced out to pasture after a certain age.

Don't let age be an excuse. Don't call anyone else elderly or old and don't classify yourself that way either. Stop acknowledging any forgetful senior moments. Aging might be inevitable but have a positive and uplifting attitude of an ol' timer who, when asked, "Have you lived here all your life?" replied, "Well, not yet."

It's been well said, "Age is mind over matter. If you don't mind, it doesn't matter." There is a wealth of experience found with those who are well-seasoned in life. There is a huge difference between growing *old* and growing *older*. Growing older is mandatory, but growing old is a choice. Growing old doesn't take any talent or ability. Grow older without growing old by always finding the opportunity to change and mature in Christ. Embrace all the stages in life since aging is inevitable. As we get older in grace we need to make the most of each day's opportunities.

A minister in his 80s was once asked, "What ten years of your life were the best?" He replied, "I haven't lived them yet." Always look ahead to the different phases of life and new opportunities to minister to one another. In the meanwhile, have fun in the Son each and every day. Enjoy the journey along the way here on earth until our final finish line with Him in heaven.

Minister to Others

An important part of our expression of Jesus to other Christians is to inspire, encourage, and edify those around us. "So let us then definitely aim for and eagerly pursue what makes for harmony and for mutual upbuilding (edification and development) of one another" (Rom. 14:19 Amp). The word "edify" comes from the word "edifice" as in a building or a structure. The pursuit of edifying others results in harmony and the mutual up-building of one another. We build up fellow believers with uplifting words and actions as expressions of encouragement.

Let's aim to inspire others to pursue the dreams God has placed in their hearts. Dreams from Him will not be accomplished if our focus remains on our personal imperfections and inadequacies. A poor self image can discourage individuals from believing that God could use them. Edification and encouragement with one another are needed to keep chasing new goals.

Real living is about continuing to grow and achieve the vision that God has given each of us no matter what our age, handicaps, or circumstances. When our dreams are lost, dying has already occurred even if we're still young in years. With no purposeful expression of Christ to one another, there are people walking around as though they are dead already and don't even know it.

> *Awake, you who sleep, Arise from the dead, And Christ will give you light. See then that you walk circumspectly, not as fools but as wise, redeeming the time, because the days are evil. Therefore do not be unwise, but understand what the will of the Lord is* (Eph. 5:14-17).

James and John were mending their nets and working when Jesus called them to follow Him. "Going on from there, He saw two other brothers, James the son of Zebedee, and John his brother, in the boat with Zebedee their father, mending their nets. He called them, and immediately they left the boat and their father, and followed Him" (Matt. 4:21-22).

In Jesus' day, fishermen would examine their nets for tangles, breaks, and weak spots that needed mending. As a fisherman's nets are designed to catch fish, we are like mended nets to become fishers of men (Matt. 4:19). In the work of our Christian expression, we are to use what we have and be equipped to be thrown out into the thick of things to fulfill God's purposes for us.

Church ought to be a place to find healing from the wounds of life. We are equipped at church services for the work of our personal expressions of ministry like nets that are mended for fishing. We are fixed, thrown out, and eventually dragged back in for more fixing. We are to all become productive joints and strategic connections that are knit together in the corporate net called the body of Christ. We are mended to mend others.

The local church is likened to a hospital full of patients in need of encouragement who find wholeness as all the patients administer their expressions of edification to one another. It is a hospital where the patients treat one another for healing. We are blessed to become a blessing. We become living epistles of the Lord's command, "Freely you have received, freely give" (Matt. 10:8).

Despite God's commands to love and encourage others, there will ever be those who have been hurt and do not want to be healed. They have a badge of honor that they will not relinquish. They do not want to give up the bitterness that is poisoning and defiling their mind and body.

Perhaps their expectation for the church may have been unrealistic and impossible to meet. What they wanted was not what they really needed. We know that our doctors care about our health, so we don't resent it when they tell us what we need to do to improve our health.

Jesus as the Great Physician calls for our obedience to continue in the teachings of His Word. If we have been hurt, His pathway to healing includes our forgiveness to uproot any emotional bitterness. After this healing process, the healed can get back in the saddle again, recommitted to their expression of ministry to bless the Lord by edifying and encouraging His Church.

Have no regret. Discover a life of fulfillment in personal ministry that puts others first. People at the end of life don't have as much regret for their actions as they do for the things they omitted doing. The only people who fear death are those with regret. We need to be an example to others in the body of Christ with our witness to the ideals for maximized personal edification.

The teachings of the New Testament repeatedly instruct us all to express, relate, and interact with each other within the body of Christ. Over fifty references are found in the epistles that contain the words "one another." Here is an alphabetical sampling of some of the "one another" verses providing a glimpse on how we are to properly demonstrate Jesus to other believers.

Admonish one another (Rom. 15:14).

Bear one another's burdens (Gal. 6:2).

Care for one another (1 Cor. 12:25).

Comfort one another (1 Thess. 4:18).

Confess your trespasses to one another (Jam. 5:16).

Having compassion for one another (1 Pet. 3:8).

Edify one another (1 Thess. 5:11).

Exhort one another daily (Heb. 3:13).

Have fellowship with one another (1 John 1:7).

Forgiving one another, just as God in Christ forgave you (Eph. 4:32).

As each one has received a gift, minister it to one another, as good stewards of the manifold grace of God (1 Pet. 4:10).

Be hospitable to one another without grumbling (1 Pet. 4:9).

Be kindly affectionate to one another with brotherly love (Rom. 12:10).

Be kind to one another (Eph. 4:32).

Be like-minded toward one another (Rom. 15:5).

Love one another (John 13:34).

Let each one of you speak truth with his neighbor, for we are members of one another (Eph. 4:25).

Have peace with one another (Mark 9:50).

Pray for one another, that you may be healed (Jam. 5:16).

In honor giving preference to one another (Rom. 12:10).

Receive one another (Rom. 15:7).

Be of the same mind toward one another (Rom. 12:16).

Through love serve one another (Gal. 5:13).

Speaking to one another in psalms and hymns and spiritual songs (Eph. 5:19).

Submitting to one another in the fear of God (Eph. 5:21).

It is quite evident that there is an abundant plethora of "one another" references found in the scriptures. This may seem to be from the Department of Redundancy department, but these scriptural instructions were inspired by the Spirit of God to motivate our expression of Him to reflect His caring nature of love and grace toward one another. Present circumstances can bring condemnation. Personal situations can feel anything but edifying. Our I'ma's can become an excuse for disqualification from our ministry of expression to serve God and one another. Some I'ma excuses include: "I'm a non-educated person." "I'm a minority." "I'm a woman." "I'm a young person." "I'm a too shy." "I'm a hurt and bitter person."

Replace the vocabulary of I'ma's with the Ican profession as in "I can do all things through Christ who strengthens me" (Phil. 4:13). All people can do all things even if they have been hurt and offended by the church. Turn to God for His ability to proclaim, "I can forgive all people through Christ who strengthens me." No matter who anyone is or what they have been through, they can mutually edify another to do all things through His strength.

Personal feelings of inadequacy or insecurity can keep a person from daring to dream the dreams God places in their heart. With the support of the Lord and one another, we can overcome any excuse that would take us out of our spiritual race. We need others in our camp to cheer us on as we all dream big together. Besides, it's not us who will be doing it anyway. It is Jesus (the strengthener within us) who will bring our expressions and dreams in Him to pass.

Be a valuable part of the Lord's entourage as His witnesses who encourage others to run with us as we joyfully finish our spiritual races together. I'm looking forward to eternity when someone will recognize my last name, Torneden, and ask, "Are you the encourager who dedicated himself to the expression of Jesus to His Church?" We are to lay aside all the excuses that would weigh us down from faithfully running our spiritual race. As we make ourselves available to the Lord and each other, our future ministry of expression to and with one another will become so bright and glorious with God that we'll all have to wear heavenly sunglasses!

CHAPTER 2

Every Joint Has To Supply

Deborah and I had just returned back to the Wichita area and were quite busy with our new positions as track coaches and teachers at Butler Community College. We were driving about thirty minutes from our home in El Dorado to attend a new upstart church in east Wichita on Sunday mornings.

For more than a year, we enjoyed the teaching ministry while sitting close to the sanctuary exit doors for our uninterrupted late arrivals and hurried departures. I was attending church services weekly (or should I say "weakly") but only in the capacity of a pew potato. I was nothing more than a non-productive, lazy spectator who did nothing but vegetate in the pew. I was only interested in being taught and ministered to by others.

Before I decided to become actively committed in allowing the Lord to use me to express His ministry to others in my local church, I had several statements down pat for my lame excuse making. It was too easy for me to respond with one of the big four excuses when asked to help: "I'm not called to do that." "I don't feel led to do that." "I'll pray about it." Or, "I don't have time."

What I was really thinking was: "It will make me uncomfortable." "My flesh doesn't want to do it." "I'll put you off and hope you don't approach me again." And, "I have the same amount of time as the next person, but I want to spend it doing other things." Such excuses limit our opportunity to exhibit an expression of Christ-likeness to one another.

The Lord began to personally deal with me with a portion of scripture,

From whom the whole body, joined and knit together by what every joint supplies, according to the effective working by which every part does its share, causes growth of the body for the edifying of itself in love (Eph. 4:16).

The phrase "every joint supplies" seemed to jump off the page of my Bible to convict me. In his writing to the church at Ephesus, the apostle Paul used several all-inclusive phrases in this one verse, "the whole body," "every joint supplies" and "every part does its share."

One Sunday morning, the Lord gently spoke to my heart with His still, small voice. He told me, "I have a promotion for you in two weeks." Right away, my mind started to race with high anticipation. This had to be something really big since He had called it "a promotion." My mind reasoned that a promotion possibly meant the position of new associate pastor.

Two Sundays later, my opportunity for promotion came exactly in the spoken time frame. After the service, I was asked if I would assist in the sound booth. That was the Lord's idea of a promotion. I faithfully helped in the sound booth and began to take on other church responsibilities during the ten years we served at that church. I made the quality decision to graduate from being an involved pew potato to an active participant totally committed to expressing Christ in my local assembly. We have a choice to be just involved or become a committed joint that provides our full supply to our local church.

Three Parables from the Kingdom of Commitment

The kingdom of commitment can be likened to a breakfast of ham and eggs. A pig and a chicken were walking by a church where a Saturday morning fundraising breakfast event was taking place. Getting caught up in the moment, the pig suggested to the chicken that they each make a contribution.

"Great idea!" the chicken exclaimed. "Let's offer them ham and eggs!"

"Not so fast," said the pig. "For you, eggs are a contribution. For me, ham is a total commitment!" The chicken was involved. The pig was committed. He who has ears to hear, let him hear.

The kingdom of commitment is compared to a Japanese kamikaze pilot in World War II assigned to make suicidal crashes into U.S. warships. (It's curious to me why these pilots motivated to kill themselves even wore helmets.) The kamikaze pilot who had completed 37 missions was involved but not committed. He who has ears to hear, let him hear.

The kingdom of commitment is also like the wife who accompanied her sick husband to the doctor's office. After the checkup, the doctor called her into his office alone.

He said, "Your husband is suffering from a serious condition, combined with horrible stress. If you don't do the following nine things, your husband will surely die. 1) Each morning, get up early and fix him a healthy breakfast. 2) Always be pleasant and make sure that he remains in a good mood. 3) For lunch, always pack him a nutritious meal to take to work. 4) And for dinner, prepare an especially nice meal for him. 5) Don't burden him with chores as this could further his stress. 6) Never discuss your problems with him as that will only make his stress worse. 7) Try to relax your husband in the evening by wearing lingerie and give him plenty of back rubs. 8) Then encourage him to watch lots of uninterrupted sporting events on television. 9) And, most importantly, make love with your husband several times a week and satisfy his every whim."

The doctor concluded, "If you can do all this non-stop for the next 10 to 12 months, there is a good chance that he will regain his health completely."

On the way home, the husband asked his wife, "What did the doctor say?" She replied, "You're going to die." This particular wife was involved but not committed. She who has ears to hear, let her hear.

I write so that you may know how you ought to conduct yourself in the house of God, which is the church of the living God, the pillar and ground of the truth (1 Tim. 3:15).

80/20 Principle

It's not reasonable to expect the unsaved or the unchurched to know how to conduct themselves in the house of God. It's a different thing, though, for those who should know better and have purposely unplugged from their proper conduct within the church of the living God. Some believers have never been actively committed to a church assembly. They sporadically attend with little involvement and no commitment for service or ministry to others.

Church administrators know of the 80/20 principle where 80 percent of the work is done by 20 percent of the people. This is a sad commentary to the non-working majority in most congregations who fail to do their share of the work at their church.

We can all learn from the responses of commitment made by the disciple Ananias, the Virgin Mary, and the apostle Paul. As they had visions from heaven, they made the right statements of obedience that we can emulate. As a committed disciple, Ananias heard the Lord speak to him and replied, "Here I am, Lord" (Acts 9:10). Mary committed herself to giving birth to God's Son and said, "Behold the maidservant of the Lord! Let it be to me according to your word" (Luke 1:38). Paul submitted his full allegiance and commitment by responding, "Lord, what do you want me to do?" (Acts 9:6).

Repeatedly in his epistles, Paul referred to himself as "the prisoner" of the Lord (Eph. 3:1). Paul laid down his life for the sake of the gospel message to the world and his ministry to the church. The Lord's committed compassion for the lost and His church constrains us to express His love toward others. Every Christian's expression is found in the action of ministering to other people.

Committed to His Will

His supernatural empowerment will flow through yielded natural vessels that are committed to do His will on this earth.

Nor [was this gift of theirs merely the contribution] that we expected, but first they gave themselves to the Lord and to us [as His agents] by the will of God, that is, entirely disregarding their personal interests, they gave as much as they possibly could, having put themselves at our disposal to be directed by the will of God (2 Cor. 8:5 Amp).

By putting ourselves at the disposal of others within the church, we are doing the will of God because we are placing His interests before any selfish personal interests.

It isn't always comfortable in the expression of commitment to perform some menial church activities, witness to strangers, or minister to the children at our church. A deny-ourselves, take-up-our-cross-and-follow-Him Christian walk wasn't meant to be comfortable anyway. Adopt a philosophy slightly altered from a presidential inauguration quote, "Ask not what your church can do for you, but what you can do for your church." His best is for His whole body to be joined and knit together as every joint supplies and every part expresses its share.

Unfortunately, there are many who lost an initial zeal for commitment to others in the church. However, it is certainly good news that the body of Christ continues to grow throughout the world. Many of these new church members initially demonstrate intensive commitment. The bad news, though, is these same active joints typically become irregular or non-attending joints after only two or three years, which makes for an enormous annual turnover.

What can be done to help new church members find their place of expression in the body of Christ and have continued joyous commitment for the rest of their lives? There are steps to take to avoid becoming a part of this alarming statistic. These saints typically drop out due to receiving an offense and to disillusionment. The church must shoulder the blame as the primary reason for the waning motivation that leads to this revolving-door syndrome.

Most everyone will be hurt by the church at one time or another. It is sad to acknowledge all the wounded joints that are now relegated to the sidelines. They were apparently not wounded by any single person or event but, as they saw it, wounded by their local church. It is like the unfortunate military casualties who were mistakenly killed by friendly fire from their own comrades during combat. They have gone from being once actively committed or perhaps overly-committed participants to now sidelined spectators as the walking wounded.

One contributing factor to friendly fire is that some churches who do not turn people toward God actually turn people away from Him through their legalism and rigid harshness. Some of these wounds are from abuse of authority, which caused people to develop a mistrust of church institutions and leadership. Because of previous disappointment, disillusionment, and past hurts, too many saints are forsaking regular church attendance.

It's a shame when many who were at one time active participants are now reduced to spectators bearing no fruit to their heavenly accounts for eternal reward. I personally grieve when considering those who were once so committed in ministering to His Church that are now totally sidelined as I.R. (Injured Reserve) because of offenses and injuries sustained by friendly fire. They are now missing opportunities for the Lord's expression to be exhorters and to receive exhortation from others.

Some of these church casualties include people who are too sensitive and easily hurt. Most of the time, this type of individual is hurt because of their own selfish expectations of what the church should do for them. They forget that what they expect the church to do for them they are not doing for others. They whine because "No one is friendly to me. No one talks to me. No one calls me."

They have no response when asked, "Are you friendly to others? Do you talk with them?" God's Word tells us, "A man who has friends must himself be friendly" (Prov. 18:24). We have to come up with gentle but firm, tough love solutions consistent with biblical teachings to help them heal from their wounds.

Appreciating One Another

The Christian church members would get along better if they learned a lesson on the expression of unity from crayons. Some crayons are sharp, some are pretty, some are dull, and some have weird names, and all are different colors. Like a computer default setting, some crayons may only see the necessity for 16 colors and not fully appreciate some of the other less primary colored crayons. From some biased crayons' perspective, peach and pumpkin are fruits, not crayon colors. And like most men, some crayons have no idea what mauve is all about. But all crayons have to learn to get along and live in the same box.

We become as faithful crayons that get along by the expression of His love. In the spirit of unity, we remain in our local church box to provide our share of color with our individual expressions of the Lord toward one another. By the unique gift of our particular color, we glorify God when every crayon does its part to create a beautiful picture. The merging of the spiritual and natural supply of all creates a divine flow together that becomes uniquely special.

The unique elements of each individual color add to what already exists in others. When the colors of red and blue merge, they make purple possible. As all the contrasting colors contribute to the work of art in progress, they help complete a perfect masterpiece. The result is a purity of brightness as each hue is at the correct gradation of color. As every crayon serves His purpose all the colors perfectly blend together to produce a brilliant expression of a portrait of Christ.

One of the mission statements in our ministry of expression to the church ought to be about developing friendships within the household of faith that last, by supporting, challenging, and loving one another. We are to "have fellowship with one another" (1 John 1:7) and to "be kindly affectionate to one another with brotherly love" (Rom. 12:10). The Lord instructed us to "have peace with one another" (Mark 9:50).

We need to decide to journey beyond the wilderness of mere involvement to the Promised Land of Commitment by living beyond ourselves. God has entrusted and assigned us to be committed to His family within our household of faith. All believers have a role and position to share in God's assembly that are uniquely valuable to the kingdom of God.

God gave the world His best with His Son. "For God so loved the world that He gave His only begotten Son, that whoever believes in Him should not perish but have everlasting life" (John 3:16). As He gave Himself to us, we are to give ourselves to Him. Jesus taught that as we give, it will be given back unto us (Luke 6:38). There is a promise of return in our giving as it will be poured back to overflowing (pressed down, shaken together, and running over), men giving unto our bosom.

When we give as supplying joints to other people, God will use others as supplying joints to give back to us. Our ministry sowing field to one another becomes our reaping field of harvest from one another. As we commit to give it our all, all will be given back in an overflowing fashion.

CHAPTER 3

Where Is My "There"?

After college, I had abruptly decided to not attend Bible school due to financial constraints caused by my lack of planning and inadequate savings. The next day, the Lord began to deal with me during my morning run. He asked me to quote Romans 12:2, which I knew was about the renewing of our minds. The Lord brought to my attention the later part of that verse, "...that good and acceptable and perfect will of God."

He made it clear that I was missing the perfect will of God with this sudden decision. Despite His warning, I justified in my mind that it was alright to settle instead for His "good" or "acceptable" will. Outside of my appointed "there," I found the next few years a spiritual wilderness experience. Nothing can compare with being in the center of God's will for our life.

In Romans 12:2, there are three distinct levels given for God's will—good, acceptable, and perfect. These three degrees of His will are like a good, a better, and a best will. A good "there" is good but not the best. An acceptable "there" is better but still not the best. His perfect "there" is divine life at its very best. We are best served to always seek Him to find a "there" which is perfect and best for us. Our desire ought to be to find His perfect will by finding His best church assembly for us.

Elijah the prophet declared to King Ahab, "As the LORD God of Israel lives, before whom I stand, there shall not be dew nor rain these years, except at my word." Then the Lord spoke to Elijah, "Get away from here and turn eastward, and hide by the Brook Cherith, which flows into the Jordan. And it will be that you shall drink from the brook, and I have commanded the ravens to feed you there" (1 Kings 17:1-4).

The Lord directed Elijah to "get away from here" to find his divinely appointed "there." God was very specific in His directions to the place of Elijah's there. God told him to "turn eastward, and hide by the Brook Cherith, which flows into the Jordan." It was not just any brook or a brook of Elijah's choice, but it was a specific brook, the "Brook Cherith." Elijah was obedient, "So he went and did according to the word of the LORD, for he went and stayed by the Brook Cherith, which flows into the Jordan" (1 Kings 17:5). Elijah not only went but then also stayed in this specific "there" until the Lord directed otherwise.

At God's "there" for Elijah, "The ravens brought him bread and meat in the morning, and bread and meat in the evening; and he drank from the brook" (1 Kings 17:6). Our "there" is where God will fulfill His covenant to supply our needs. The Hebrew word translated *Cherith* means "to cut." It comes from a root word which means "to covenant by cutting flesh and passing between the pieces." God was making a covenant with Elijah in his "there" at a place called Cherith to take care of all his needs by sending bread and meat (today's equivalent of quarter-pounders minus the fat calories) by ravens twice daily.

God will direct every believer to their own local church, a "there" to provide spiritual sustenance. Our church and our pastor is our Brook Cherith of God's selection. It is His choice of brooks not ours. At God's divinely appointed "there," He will supply all our provisions through a covenant of obedience as we respond to the word of the Lord.

What happened next for Elijah may also happen to us. God may lead us from our place that becomes a "here" even though it was previously our "there." "And it happened after a while that the brook dried up, because there had been no rain in the land" (1 Kings 17:7). Our "here" is no longer God's "there" when that brook goes dry and a hunger for more consumes us.

Elijah was later hiding in a cave while running from Jezebel. The Lord asked him twice, "What are you doing here, Elijah?" (1 Kings 19:9,13). Then in verse 19, we see that Elijah departed from that "here" and got back into God's will when he went on to his appointed "there." When God speaks to our heart, "What are you doing here?" it's time to move on to an even better "there." God expects us to be willing to be stretched by moving on in His will to discover our God-appointed "there."

The word of the Lord had come to Elijah clearly directing him to the Brook Cherith. Later, the brook that once sustained him dried up. Then the word of the Lord came to him, saying, "Arise, go to Zarephath, which belongs to Sidon, and dwell there. See, I have commanded a widow there to provide for you" (1 Kings 17:8,9). God directed Elijah to another "there" called Zarephath. God told him of a widow "there" who would provide for him. Initially, Cherith provided his needs, but things changed over time. The Lord may direct us to another "there"—for example, another church home even though the previous church was indeed His selected place for a season.

It will be recognizable when our "here" is not God's desired "there." In some cases, it can be quite obvious. For example, it would be highly recommended to rapidly depart any church that uses the "Dr. Seuss Version Bible" where Jesus fed the thousands by multiplying green eggs and ham. A hasty exit is also in order if there is an ATM in the foyer, or if the ushers ask, "Smoking or non-smoking?"

God will speak to listening hearts to provide an assembly of believers that meets all our spiritual needs. "Your ears shall hear a word behind you, saying, 'This is the way, walk in it,' whenever you turn to the right hand or whenever you turn to the left" (Isaiah 30:21). God will speak and guide us to our appointed "there" to be fed and ministered to.

Suddenly or gradually, things change, dry up, and don't seem right for us anymore. His grace that was once at our "there" has lifted. He is no longer in our current "here." The children of Israel would obediently follow "by day in a pillar of cloud to lead the way, and by night in a pillar of fire to give them light" (Ex. 13:21). When God moved, they moved. When God stayed, they stayed. The key is a willingness to seek Him for His direction in finding God's "there" for each of us.

Jacob had a life-altering experience when he was alone with God at a specific place called Peniel. There the Lord "wrestled with him" and "blessed him there" (Gen. 32:24-30). Blessings come when we seeking His face at our "there." We are to seek God with the motive of knowing Him more intimately to find His will for us.

There are some who only spend time alone with God when they need to seek His hand rather than His face. The best blessings come when we seek the face of the Blesser not just His blessings. We touch His heart with our sincere devotion to know and please Him. As we demonstrate the right priorities to diligently seek Him and His kingdom, then the blessings of the things being added unto us will surely follow (Heb. 11:6; Matt. 6:33).

Jacob's character was transformed for the better as God wrestled with him at a "there" he called Peniel, which means "the face of God." Our open hearts become a "there" place of prayer, visitation from God, and a habitation that changes the condition of our heart. At his "there," God wrestled with Jacob and touched the hollow of his thigh to break his fleshly strength and resistance. Jacob came to that place as a supplanter, schemer, trickster, and swindler but returned as Israel or a contender with God. In God's presence, Jacob's deceiving nature was changed. Seeking God's face and submitting to His love at our "there" is the place where we will find our destiny and potential in Him. At our "there," God can turn us from Jacobs into Israels.

The cry of our hearts is to ever seek fresh manna from heaven

21

since yesterday's manna will become stale and wanting. To live two consecutive days on the same spiritual plane is a disappointment. It becomes a travesty for us to become stationary and settled in our spirituality. Each day is a place of choice. Every day is an opportunity for spiritual advancement.

Inner Revival

We need to come to the place where we are no longer living just for ourselves but are living a daily life that is continually renewed and refreshed by His indwelling Spirit. There we will enjoy a perpetual lifestyle of continual inner revival within and without. The goal is to "be strong in the Lord—be empowered through your union with Him; draw your strength from Him—that strength which His [boundless] might provides" (Eph. 6:10 Amp).

It is the tendency of human nature to resist change and to stay in a "here" called "the Brook Comfort Zone, which flows into the Boredom" (1 Fred 17:3). We need to change the way we view change. The one constant about walking with God is change. Change is unavoidable in a life with God. We need to come to the place of an ever-changing all the time. When we are through changing, then we are through. In nature, anything that remains stagnant all the time is either dead or on the verge of dying. As we stay flexible and make heart adjustments, His grace will bring lasting change. Seek His change by resisting fixed and stationary positions that are nothing more than old manna and monuments to past experiences.

Only the Lord knows what waits in the future for the obedient. Shortly before His ascension, Jesus told an assembly of believers to tarry in Jerusalem—their appointed "there"—to be endued with power from on high (Luke 24:49; Acts 1:8). Five hundred were present to hear His command but sadly, ten days later, only 120 remained to receive the power of the Holy Ghost's outpouring on the Day of Pentecost (1 Cor. 15:6; Acts 1:15). What happened to the other 380? Over 75% of the congregation were not at their appointed "there" and missed out on God's best for them that day in the upper room. We need to diligently seek God for His best and perfect will. We cannot be fully used for His glory until we have found our best and perfect church assembly.

We shouldn't be alarmed or disappointed when a perfect God puts us in His perfect will at our perfect "there" with an imperfect pastor and an imperfect congregation. Since each of us is imperfect, it's unrealistic to expect everything in our assembly to be perfect. After all, only perfect sheep deserve a perfect church with a perfect pastor. Even if there were a perfect church, it would all come to an end as soon as we walked through the door.

A comedian once said he wouldn't want to belong to any club that would have him as a member. We belong to imperfect clubs called local churches with imperfect people. God brought us to our "there" to assist with making that assembly more perfect. God has an assembly—a "there"—for every believer's ministry to the body of Christ. As with Elijah, our "there" is a specific place to where God will direct us.

And let us consider and give attentive, continuous care to watching over one another, studying how we may stir up (stimulate and incite) to love and helpful deeds and noble activities; not forsaking or neglecting to assemble together [as believers], as is the habit of some people, but admonishing— warning, urging and encouraging—one another, and all the more faithfully as you see the day approaching (Heb. 10:24,25 Amp).

Encourage One Another

The habit of some people in forsaking and neglecting to assemble together causes missed opportunities for their ministry to consider and give attentive, continuous care to admonish, warn, urge, and encourage one another. We are all to consider our place of assembly as a local church for ministry where we attend to exhort one another. We are all ministers of exhortation instructed to consider one another for good works, helpful deeds, and noble activities which glorify Him.

Absent from their assembly, believers cannot stir up, stimulate, or incite His love. Those that forsake and are negligent in their church attendance become like stagnant pools with limited outlets to give out to other believers. As local churches assemble together, every Christian present have the privilege of ministering corporately as they consider one another by admonishing one another.

The assembling of believers is the time to express the three C's—care, comfort, and compassion. We are to "care for one another" (1 Cor. 12:25), "comfort one another" (1 Thess. 4:18) and have "compassion for one another" (1 Pet. 3:8). We come to give and receive His expressions of compassion as we care for and comfort one another.

"Be mindful to be a blessing, especially to those of the household of faith—those who belong to God's family with you, the believers" (Gal. 6:10 Amp). We cannot be a blessing to the "household of faith" when we habitually miss services at our church. To stay home from church services and only receive ministry from television or radio ministries are not God's best.

Serving the Lord is about following the instructions in His Word to minister to one another at our appointed "there." God is pleased with our obedience that demonstrates His love for each one. As the body of Christ becomes mindful of proper relationships with one another, unity within the community of local churches and ministries will be achieved. The greatest personal fulfillment for a Christian comes with finding their place at their "there" to both give and receive the wealth of ministry gifts found in His body, the church.

CHAPTER 4

In God's Eyes

As a family of four with two young boys, we would playfully joke with one another about how we're pushing each other's buttons. Our sons, Kyle and Myles, would join in on the fun and poke each other's sides laughing, "I'm pushing your buttons." There is an art to the expression of meaningful touch in our relationships where we purposely attempt to touch all the right buttons with one another.

During World War II, a classic study on this subject was done in a European orphanage where the infant death rate was astronomically high. In an attempt to reverse the horrible trend, researchers scheduled nurses to hold and touch the babies on a regular basis. The results were amazing, as the infants responded to their loving touches by clinging to life. God created man with a need to give and receive love through all five of the senses.

Our oldest son, Kyle, is our special miracle boy who was born three months premature. Kyle weighed only one pound seven ounces at birth. He has done extremely well considering the high death rates and chances of health issues associated with preemies born that early. Deborah would spend about eight hours a day in the hospital talking, praying, and touching Kyle during his first eighty days in intensive care. His doctor commented how Kyle always did better than he should have. Our loving touches and faith in a loving God who answers prayer made the difference in his recovery.

All parents comment on how quickly their children grow up. Deborah has purposed to enjoy every moment with our two sons.

She has never looked past the present in anticipation of hurrying them toward future development. Deborah has savored every opportunity to relish all of the once-in-a-lifetime experiences with opportunities for affirming touches with our children.

All fathers ought to be encouraged—even while their children are small babies—to be actively committed to their development. It's important to play with them. When little girls become preteens and teens, don't stop hugging them. Deborah appreciates it when I'm on the floor playfully wrestling with our boys like her father did when she and her siblings were growing up. Appropriate and affirming touches offer security and communicate love, appreciation, and fondness.

His compassion for others will well up within as we purpose to see one another in God's eyes. The richest living is to make it a priority to develop our relationships with those around us. Pour into one another by becoming a sphere of influence for a quality effect on the development of others. Put into practice the ripple style of relational ministry where small circles of influence spread into larger ones. Our influence of love upon our immediate circles will assist others in their circles in maturing to the point where they too become positive influencers within their circles of love.

The eyes of the Lord beheld and considered the discipleship potential of the rich, young ruler. "Then Jesus beholding him loved him" (Mark 10:21 KJV). We are to see the people of the world and one another within the church with His eyes. A love walk includes beholding and embracing the people God brings across our paths.

Concentrating on One Another

To behold another is to be fully centered on that person in that moment of time. Our total concentration will make him or her feel like the most important person in the room. People with that kind of focus have a high recall of names because their concentration is more on the other person than on themselves. Other people will know when the beholder genuinely cares. As the saying goes, they will not care how much we know until they know how much we care.

Psychologists tell us that few things communicate love more powerfully than to actually pay attention to other people when we're with them. The classic opposite of this is the father who can't stop watching sports on television long enough to find out how his son's day went or the mother who keeps one eye on a newspaper article while her teenage daughter talks about her social life at school. Relationships can't thrive this way. Focused attention is important.

We were having difficulties with our young son Myles who was not immediately obeying our requests. One day in frustration I asked him, "Did you hear what I just said?" There was silence. Then it occurred to me that he was not being disobedient. He was just in his own little boy world and not listening.

Later, he was noisily chattering to himself and his brother in the backseat of our car as we were driving to church. Deborah asked him to quiet down, but a few moments later he became even louder. Finally, she asked him, "What did I just tell you?" After a brief pause, Myles responded, "To stop doing something?"

We later found a t-shirt for him that said, "Can you repeat the part after 'Listen carefully'?"

When we're with people, we need to really be there. People will respond and feel listened to when they're looked in the eye and beheld with His love. Jesus was moved with compassion as He "saw" the multitudes with the Father's great love. "But when He saw the multitudes, He was moved with compassion for them, because they were weary and scattered, like sheep having no shepherd" (Matt. 9:36).

The crowds were drawn to Jesus because He did not see them for their skin color or whether they were rich or poor, male or female, old or young. Jesus, as the Father God's love representative, treated everyone with no partiality. As God is no respecter of persons (Acts 10:34 KJV), neither should we have any prejudice or practiced favoritism. We need to learn to be sensitive to His leading on how to love impartially.

The Lord Jesus raised the dead, healed the sick, and walked on water, yet He gladly accepted the lesser folks who were common fisherman and sinful prostitutes. He radiated so much love for the people that they would swarm Him. They felt good about themselves in His presence.

Our oldest son, Kyle, has always been a visual person with great attention to detail. From his childhood, Kyle has also had tremendous sensitivity for the well-being of others. His sincere concern for others and their infirmities at such a young age has been an inspiration. His compassion for other people is truly a gift from God.

Brothers and Sisters

Like our Lord, we need to view one another in our local church as dear brothers and sisters in a family of believers related by His shed blood. We are all joint heirs together in Him with equal rights and responsibilities. It is important to treat everyone with respect and make them feel valued. We need to attentively listen to them when they are talking and not judge in a critical fashion. A true love walk will treat all people the same even if there is no personal gain or interest in developing a relationship.

The Lord God said, "It is not good that man should be alone; I will make him a helper comparable to him" (Gen. 2:18). God acknowledged that it was not good for mankind to be without companions. Relational people understand the importance of our innate need for companionship with God and with one another. Companionship is a very precious commodity because it can only be bought with the one thing that seems to be so scarce—our time. We must spend plenty of time with another to develop a relationship. An effective, relational Christian has time for those around them. Without adequate time, we will miss important moments and opportunities to build lasting relationships that bond.

Relationship Building

We need to make the time for our immediate family and for the household of faith. Our culture addresses the differences between *quality* time and *quantity* time. The truth is both are needed to build bonding relationships through intentional planning. What we purposefully write into our schedules is what we will really do. We should determine that relationships matter most in life and schedule time for that before work and other obligations take over.

Relationally oriented people think differently from persons who are task-oriented. The latter put their assigned tasks as a priority before their relationships with people. They will walk right through a group of people and not say a word because of their mission to get their tasks completed. A relational man or woman will walk slowly through that same crowd and interact with everyone, thereby demonstrating God's love and their valued importance.

The task-driven person may truly love people, but what good is that love if it is not clearly demonstrated? Those who have task-oriented tendencies should make it their goal to develop better relational skills and change their priorities.

Unification within the church is marked by relationship building. The first relationship to be enjoyed is continued fellowship with our Father God through His Son Jesus by the Holy Spirit. Our heavenly Father, Jesus, and the Holy Spirit were seeking fellowship and companionship when they agreed, "Let Us [Father, Son, and Holy Spirit] make mankind in Our image, after Our likeness" (Gen. 1:26 Amp). In the Garden of Eden, God really enjoyed walking in the cool of the day with His creation called man. God prefers to not be alone without His man as He invites "whosoever will" as the criterion for the mailing list to His banquet feast in heaven.

Jesus tells His church, "Behold, I stand at the door and knock. If anyone hears My voice and opens the door, I will come in to him and dine with him, and he with Me" (Rev. 3:20). He is always there within our hearts for immediate companionship. He comforts us with the words, "I will never leave you nor forsake you" (Heb. 13:5). The Lord fulfills His and our tremendous need for fellowship. Likewise, He expects each of us to be companions who fellowship with His people.

Jesus acknowledged our value to God the Father, "I have manifested Your name to the men whom You have given Me out of the world. They were Yours, You gave them to Me, and they have kept Your word" (John 17:6). Jesus views us as gifts given to Him by His Father. Having the same attitude, relationally oriented people view others placed in their lives as precious gifts from God.

In His earthly ministry, Jesus would not have sent an angelic scroll to the Father stating, "I have completed my tasks here. Please note the turning water into wine, multiplying loaves and fishes, healing the sick, and raising the dead." His memo probably would have gone more like, "Father, as proof of my good work here, I present to you Peter, John, James … Mary Magdalene, Martha, and Lazarus. All completed in love." People are the reason for ministry. Our expressions of His love to other people are life's greatest accomplishments as the trophies that we'll take with us from earth to heaven.

Communication

Though Jesus taught and healed the multitudes, fed the thousands by multiplying the loaves and fishes, and sent out the seventy, He poured Himself into those special twelve. In Mark 4:34, we read, "And when they were alone, He explained all things to His disciples." Two chapters later, we see this communication reciprocated, "Then the apostles gathered to Jesus and told Him all things, both what they had done and what they had taught" (Mark 6:30). In those two scriptures, we see precedence for us to emulate our Lord with close relationships similar to Jesus and the twelve who had strong verbal communication in sharing "all things." Our Lord lived closely with His disciples and called them "My friends" (John 15:14-15).

Communication is not just talking. Communication means both talking and listening. Most children will tell us they hate to be lectured to but love to be listened to. The only way communication happens is for us to ask questions and listen—not only for the words but for the true meaning behind the words. We should behold with the Lord's eyes while listening with God's heart.

This is a sharp contrast to the management styles in some businesses today. There is a comical quote of a real boss who said, "We know that communication is a problem, but the company is not going to discuss it with any of the employees."

Transparent people who are full of joy will have nothing to hide as they serve others with God's expressions of love. If they are who they claim to be, people should respect them the closer they get. The principle of service is what separates true ministry from glory seeking. "Through love serve one another" (Gal. 5:13). To love is to serve. Effective, close relationships will build love and loyalty. We do not want to lose sight of life's true meaning of sacrificing ourselves for the sakes of others.

Jesus set the example of serving His disciples and those who followed Him. He seemed to have no boundaries as far as His group was concerned. The Lord welcomed children. He was criticized by the religious establishment for socializing with sinners, prostitutes, and tax collectors. Jesus was invited to their parties as He played with and enjoyed the people. We can sense from the scriptures that Jesus reflected joy and laughter, causing the people to flock to Him.

Jesus poured Himself into a rag-tag group of unlikely future apostles who were totally human and certainly not divine. In spite of their illiteracy, shaky backgrounds, reeking of the smell of fish, divisive tendencies, and momentary cowardice, our Lord pushed all the right buttons to create an environment for a successfully laid foundation where eleven of His twelve "apostle projects" went on in their individual and corporate ministries that established the early church. The Lord brought the heaven out of those eleven.

Jesus gave us an example of how our ministry of His expression through us toward one another is about beholding and influencing others. He so transformed those individuals that they went on to radically change the world for His glory. We need to behold the others around us with His eyes and His heart to sense their potential in Christ. From the Lord's perspective, let's allow Him to reveal creative ways to love and push the buttons that will bring God's best out of other Christians.

CHAPTER 5

Our Divine Hookups

Our overly excited cross country team was back inside our school van. As a junior college squad, we had just stunned the University of Arkansas by winning the 1997 Hurricane Festival hosted by the University of Tulsa. In cross country scoring, the first five finishers receive points based on place as the lowest score wins. A perfect score would be 15 points for placing five scorers in the first five places. We scored a near-perfect 19 points to Arkansas' 39 points in winning the five-team meet.

The cross country and track tradition at Arkansas is truly legendary. At that time they had won more NCAA national championships than any other team in any other sport in the history of college athletics. We were only one of two teams to beat the Razorbacks that fall. The Arkansas men's program didn't lose again that season until a close second place finish to Stanford at the NCAA National Cross Country Championships.

I knew that the Razorbacks had trained through this early season meet without expecting anyone to challenge them, especially a two-year college. I realized that this was a special day for our program unlikely to ever happen again. I had waited until we were away from the other teams and inside the small confines of our 15-passenger van. I surprised everyone when I asked them all to be quiet for a moment of silence. After pausing for a few seconds, I unexpectedly screamed to the top of my lungs in celebration. We all roared in laughter.

I shared a different kind of experience with our team two years before. I found myself a bit subdued even though we had just won the 1995 NJCAA National Cross Country Championships where I was selected National Coach of the Year. As we were driving back to the hotel, one of our athletes challenged me as to why I wasn't showing more outward emotion. I tried my best to articulate to them that I was certainly thrilled that we had accomplished our goal, but that it had just hit me that our journey together was now over. I had enjoyed our camaraderie so much that I felt an emotional letdown with the realization that our season together had reached completion. This was a special group of men who would also finish as the first academic team nationally. The process had been so wonderful with this group that I was disappointed for it all to end.

So much in life is missed without an appreciation to nurture and fully develop all our potential relationships and friendships. Life's richest pleasure is the mutual journey of fellowship with God and other Christians. There's more to just being driven to reach a goal. Where is the accomplishment if we have climbed to the top of the mountain of success and then have no one with whom to share the experience? It is amiss to be so focused on our destination that we don't fully treasure the journey with those around us. Our focus shouldn't be only on the goal but on the process of fulfilling that goal.

Barnabas, Son of Encouragement

In the book of Acts, Joses was a positive influencer for the Lord. "And Joses, who was also named Barnabas by the apostles (which is translated Son of Encouragement), a Levite of the country of Cyprus, having land, sold it, and brought the money and laid it at the apostles' feet" (Acts 4:36-37). Joses was renamed Barnabas by the apostles, which name means "son of encouragement."

Some traditions teach that Barnabas was the rich, young ruler who Jesus beheld and loved. If this were indeed true, it is a great story of redemption of how he belatedly gave all his possessions to follow the Lord Jesus to become the "son of encouragement" to express God's love to the church.

In the book of Acts, the encourager Barnabas was the one who saw the potential in the new convert named Saul. Church leadership didn't trust Saul because he had recently been responsible for the arrest and murder of many Christians. Barnabas later went to Tarsus and found Saul isolated in the wilderness. Barnabas brought him back to the local church at Antioch so he could develop his ministerial teaching gift. Saul found his place in that church and from there was promoted to his next phase of ministry.

Our ministerial supply of expression will be both received and given within our community of believers. We all have crucial divine relationships that we need to discover within the body of Christ. Without their encouragement and influence, we will not reach our full potential in our ministry to one another. After Barnabas and Saul fulfilled their ministry as faithful prophets and teachers at the church at Antioch, God promoted and sent them both forth as apostles to the Gentiles (Acts 12:25).

Now in the church that was at Antioch there were certain prophets and teachers: Barnabas, Simeon who was called Niger, Lucius of Cyrene, Manaen who had been brought up with Herod the tetrarch, and Saul. As they ministered to the Lord and fasted, the Holy Spirit said, "Now separate to Me Barnabas and Saul for the work to which I have called them." Then, having fasted and prayed, and laid hands on them, they sent them away (Acts 13:1-3).

These ministers came together corporately to minister to the Lord while in the church that was at Antioch. It is in our church—our God-designated Antioch—where we will find our own company to flow with. God has special divine relationships for all of us. His plan for us is to minister alongside our glorious connections.

Barnabas took the early leadership role in this dynamic duo

ministerial partnership (Acts 11:30). Due to Barnabas' encouragement, Saul's ministry gifts would mature so that he later became Paul, the heralded apostle to the Gentile world. Paul then stepped into the leadership role and became the primary speaker for the team (Acts 13:13; Acts 14:12). Their divine hookup had an incredible impact as together they ministered and preached the gospel to previously unreached parts of the world.

Later, the encourager Barnabas wanted to give a supportive associate minister named Mark another opportunity. Mark had previously quit and left for home during their first mission trip together. Paul was so animatedly opposed to Barnabas' willingness to give Mark another chance, that this glorious association parted ways.

After their separation, Paul traveled with Silas while Barnabas took young Mark under his wing of encouragement. It seems unfortunate when we consider that Barnabas is never mentioned again after this split. This is probably due mostly to the fact that Luke—the author of the book of Acts—was one of Paul's supportive ministers and traveling partner.

We do, however, later see the fruit of the Barnabas' mentoring of this young minister. Barnabas' decision proved true as Mark's development as a minister was evident. Paul had a change of heart later expressed in a letter to Timothy, "Only Luke is with me. Get Mark and bring him with you, for he is useful to me for ministry" (2 Tim. 4:11). Without Barnabas' encouragement, Mark would have not matured to the point of usefulness in the ministry of the gospel.

We are like Barnabas when we seek out the Sauls and the Marks whom God will place into our path. As encouragers, we can help fellow ministers find their place in the church and fulfill their call in the passion, purpose, and plan of God. One of our personal ministerial goals is to build up those of the body of Christ around us. We are to "admonish one another" (Rom. 15:14) and "exhort one another daily" (Heb. 3:13). As a part of the true remnant of extreme encouragers, we can make a difference with one another as there are already enough discouraging people in the world and unfortunately, in the church.

Encouragement is a two-way street. Church leadership is not only the ministers charged to encourage others. All the members of a church are to recognize and esteem very highly those whom the Great Shepherd has placed to watch over them as faithful under-shepherds of His flock (1 Thess. 5:12-13). Under-shepherds and pastoral teams need encouragement as do all people. We can mutually encourage and exhort one another. We need to receive and encourage the covering of a pastoral staff placed over us as we do our Barnabas friends around us.

We Need One Another

Our ability to love and develop proper friendships with other people begins first with our relationship with God. Our degree of love for Jesus will be measured proportionately with our love for our brethren. To profess to be partners with God but not with other Christian saints who also have the same God in them is a grave mistake. It is subtle pride to say, "I don't need other Christians, a local church, or a pastor" or "I only need Jesus." Our ministry of expression should be to both Jesus and our divine hookup relationships.

One of the goals of the church is to embrace a ministry that does not promote legalistic or religious works but where all presentations of the Word are based on the intimate knowledge of and the personal fellowship and relationship with our heavenly Father, the Lord Jesus, and the Holy Spirit. In that context, our desire should be to institute a personable leadership philosophy where the saints exhibit quality interpersonal relationships.

We all benefit from the personal interaction of our Christian friendships. "As iron sharpens iron, So a man sharpens the countenance of his friend" (Prov. 27:17). Friends don't let friends go unsharpened. The indicator of true unity in community is the quality of our relationships with our own company of Christian friends.

An important characteristic of stable Christians is whether they have kept or maintained close relationships with other believers for a long period of time. Wisdom and common sense dictate to never fully trust anybody who cannot maintain long-term friendships. Likewise, watch Christians who are so unstable that they are constantly offended, upset, and switching churches every few months with every whim. They are obviously lacking in the area of maintaining faithfulness in nurturing lasting relationships with the shepherd and church that God has called them to.

When an individual has old friends in their life, it reveals that that person has learned to keep peace, forgive when offended, and accept differences in others. Commitment has been both learned and valued by such individuals. God expects us to exhibit love and commitment among best friends. This is the foundation of strength in the local church.

In the past, there has been preaching and negative comments made toward natural cliques in our churches due to the exclusive behavior of some. It is counter-productive though to come against cliques because they actually serve to unite a local church. The building block of unity is homogeneous units—family and like-minded people—who comprise a church body.

Jesus could have been accused of forming His own clique. Though Jesus ministered to the multitudes, the majority of His time was spent with the twelve disciples. Even within that small select dozen, there was the inner circle of Peter, John, and James. Only those three had the special opportunity to accompany our Lord to the mount of transfiguration, to raise Jairus' daughter from death, and to pray at Gethsemane.

Did Jesus love the inner three more than the other nine? The answer is obviously no. He was aware of all their destinies and allowed them closer access to Himself for their training and ministerial education. This would seem to be an exclusive clique gathering but yet it is our example in the scriptures.

Obviously, we can't be best buddies with everyone. There are going to be people with whom we will automatically click with. God has those people with whom we are to be best friends while still being friendly with everyone else. We all should meet new people and welcome first-time guests into our congregations. We can make new friends while at the same time cultivating and maintaining deep, long-term friendships.

This bonding is what brings unity in our Christian community as the necessity of tight-knit groups will give mutual support in the body of Christ. These groups are an integral part of creating unity and building the church. As we locate our own company with our divine hookups, the Holy Ghost will provide His chemistry to establish a church community that displays love, unity, and power.

We will actually miss out if we neglect to find our destined buddies in the Lord to be blessed and to be a blessing. We are a ministry gift from God to bless others. We are channels through which His grace flows. We can become rivers of His unconditional favor and impartial love flowing through us to others. Our emphasis becomes us to them and not just them to us.

We all ought to have some tight relationships that have meaning. In our lives, there are many casual relationships but only a handful of intimate ones. There are a few significant relationships to the kingdom of God who are our special divine ones. God sends these special glorious connections to help encourage and strengthen our walk with Him. Don't miss any God-sent Barnabas-like divine relationships. They are destined to be our fellow laborers. Such divine relationships are few and far between.

Paul wrote,

*Then after fourteen years I went up again to Jerusalem with
Barnabas, and also took Titus with me. And I went up by revelation, and communicated to them that gospel which I preach
among the Gentiles, but privately to those who were of reputation, lest by any means I might run, or had run, in vain....
And when James, Cephas, and John, who seemed to be pillars,
perceived the grace that had been given to me, they gave me
and Barnabas the right hand of fellowship, that we should go to
the Gentiles and they to the circumcised* (Gal. 2:1-2,9).

Paul describes his relationship with the apostolic brethren in
Jerusalem as he met with "those who were of reputation" to communicate his ministry and the gospel he preached to insure that his
race was not run in vain. James, Peter and John had been together a
long time and were cherished friends. These "pillars" were inviting
Paul and Barnabas to step into their intimate circle of friendship.

This invitation for Paul to join them was a great sign that they
approved of him personally and respected the work of ministry in
his life. When the apostles gave Paul the right hand of fellowship,
they were not inviting him over for mere small talk. They were
opening the door for Paul to enter their sanctum of tender and
intimate fellowship with one another.

Thanks to the encouragement of Barnabas, Saul was transformed into Paul. Right after his conversion, Saul was not fully
trusted initially by the apostles. But thanks to Barnabas, Paul was
later welcomed into a divine relationship built on intimate, meaningful communion based on absolute trust.

God has plans for all of us that include our own company,
groups, companions, and friends. We are to pour ourselves into
those destined to be at our side. Enjoy, cherish, and relish them. I
had a friend who was a personal project of mine once tell me in
appreciation, "Thanks for being a Barnabas to me this past year."
His heartfelt comment meant much to me but more importantly, I
believe it also meant even more to my Lord.

God has ordained divine hookups for every one of us. God will place key people around us for encouragement. These are people who are to be in the same flow as we are. The most wonderful part of life's journey is the special relationships we savored along the way. We should appreciate, partner up with, and cultivate a close relationship with our glorious associations. Be a Barnabas who gives to and receives from your Barnabas' friends. Enjoy life at its best by realizing that people are God's greatest gifts to us. The greatest gift we can give ourselves is a friend. Open all the Barnabas gifts that the Great Giver has given to each and every one of us.

CHAPTER 6

Dare 2 Care

My sermon illustrations from the pulpit are often personal stories that I love to share about fun times in our family life. When our young boys say amusing things, I think of when Jesus said, "Have you never read, 'Out of the mouth of babes?'" (Matt. 21:16). Many life lessons can be taught from what proceeds out of the mouths of young children. Of course it seems most precious when those babes are our own.

When our son Kyle was four, he came running into my home office. He was just back from shopping with his mother for my birthday presents. In his excitement, he whispered, "Sh-h-h, it's a secret. We got you blue underwear. Don't tell anyone 'cause it's a secret!"

At that evening's church service, Kyle was quick to tell the entire congregation about his secret concerning the color of their pastor's new underwear.

As we fully discover our Christian expression of ministry, we cannot keep a secret of the greatest message to be communicated to the world. Just before His ascension to heaven, Jesus made this final proclamation to the church,

> *All authority has been given to Me in heaven and on earth.... Go into all the world and preach the gospel to every creature. He who believes and is baptized will be saved; but he who does not believe will be condemned.... Go therefore and make disciples of all the nations* (Matthew 19:18; Mark 16:15-16; Matthew 19:19).

Ministering and Serving

His purpose in the expression of ministry is for participants not spectators. The church can be compared to a football game with thousands of spectators in the stands with a desperate need for exercise and 22 players on the field in a desperate need for rest. The proclamation of this good news is the participant ministry of every believer.

Many workers in the church are running rampant with busyness yet without the priority of purpose. Many work IN the church without doing the work OF the church? Their work in A church might not necessarily be the work of THE church. In our busyness in administrative details and the tasks of ministry, we can lose sight of the fact that people are to be the emphasis of every Christian's expression.

Our ministry certainly includes our service to one another within the church. But there is also an important ministry for all of us outside the church. The work OF the church isn't confined within the four walls. The church's primary purpose is about going and sending to preach the gospel to the entire world. It's THE work and THE purpose of the church to seek out God's lost creation.

James A. Garfield was the first ambidextrous president of the United States. He was also a minister and an elder of the Christian Church. Before beginning a distinguished career in the military and politics, Garfield had brief stints as first a preacher and then as an instructor in classical languages. It is reported that one could ask him a question in English, and he could simultaneously write the answer in Latin with one hand and Ancient Greek with the other.

Every Christian is to have similar versatility in the expressing of their ministry. With equal ease, we are each to use ambidexterity in expression by ministering both within the church and without the church. Our ministry is two-fold. We are to demonstrate His love to one another in our local church and take the gospel message to those we come in contact with outside the four walls of our church.

When Adam fell in the garden, it wasn't Adam but God who suffered the greatest loss. God lost the man who had walked with Him in the cool of the day to hiding in fear and sin. From the time God called out to Adam, "Where are you?" He had a plan to redeem a fallen mankind by His loving kindness, justice, and righteousness. God created man for fellowship and He wants His creation back through His redemptive plan of salvation. We are to be His Redeem Team who expresses His gospel of redemption to the entire world.

God's plan and purpose for Jesus is expressed beautifully in the Amplified translation of the most famous verse in the Bible, "God so greatly loved and dearly prized the world that He [even] gave up His only begotten (unique) Son, so that whoever believes in (trusts, clings to, relies on) Him shall not perish—come to destruction, be lost—but have eternal (everlasting) life" (John 3:16 Amp).

The plan for His purpose for us centers upon His great love for the people in this world. He dearly prized the world and gave His Son as a sacrifice to atone for the sin that separated mankind from His glory and presence. The priority for His church is to proclaim this message of peace and goodwill toward men (Luke 2:14).

When each believer is born again in Christ as a new creation in Him, he or she is immediately given the ministry of reconciliation.

Therefore, if anyone is in Christ, he is a new creation; old things have passed away; behold, all things have become new. Now all things are of God, who has reconciled us to Himself through Jesus Christ, and has given us the ministry of reconciliation, that is, that God was in Christ reconciling the world to Himself, not imputing their trespasses to them, and has committed to us the word of reconciliation (2 Cor. 5:17-19).

Reconciliation

God Himself has committed to the entire church to express this word of reconciliation. To every believer He has given the ministry of reconciliation. Our Lord has entrusted us with preaching the gospel that determines each person's eternal destiny. Those who believe will be saved, and those who have not been told or who do not believe will be damned (Mark 16:16). It is a sobering thought when we consider that other people's blood will be on the hands of those who do not take part in preaching the gospel to the world.

God has established us as His adopted children to reach the world with His glorious gospel. He cares through us, loves through us, and heals through us. We are His hands, His feet, and His mouthpiece to this world.

Our Lord's priority and purpose is easily recognized when considering His first and last words recorded in the book of Mark. He first said to his disciples, "Follow Me, and I will make you become fishers of men" (Mark 1:16-18). They immediately left their fishing nets and followed Him for greater fish to catch. Before His ascension, His final words to His disciples were, "Go into all the world and preach the gospel to every creature" (Mark 16:15). With God, everything starts and finishes with His purpose to make us all fishers of men who preach the gospel of reconciliation in Christ.

It is a wise mindset to make priority one the primary purpose of missions, the harvest and soul-winning. "The fruit of the righteous is a tree of life, And he who wins souls is wise" (Prov. 11:30).

The church at large needs to be informed that over three billion people in the world have not yet heard the gospel. These billions are unreached, lost, helpless, and vulnerable to the devil's attacks. It is not right that a few should hear the gospel many times when so many have not heard it even once. So many are looking forward to His second coming when over half the world has yet to hear about His first coming. Everyone has a right to hear the glorious gospel before they die or Christ triumphantly returns.

The gospel of Christ is the power of God to salvation for everyone who believes. The true Bible gospel is a message of peace, grace, mercy, and hope. The Bible gospel is the simple message of God's plan of salvation for all mankind.

The essence and simplicity of the true gospel is found in 1 Corinthians 15:1-4,

> *Moreover, brethren, I declare to you the gospel which I preached to you, which also you received and in which you stand, by which also you are saved, if you hold fast that word which I preached to you — unless you believed in vain. For I delivered to you first of all that which I also received: that Christ died for our sins according to the Scriptures, and that He was buried, and that He rose again the third day according to the Scriptures."*

His glorious gospel found here is threefold: to preach to all that Christ died for our sins, He was buried, and He rose again. To receive this gift of salvation, Paul writes

> *If you confess with your mouth the Lord Jesus and believe in your heart that God has raised Him from the dead, you will be saved. For with the heart one believes unto righteousness, and with the mouth confession is made unto salvation. For the Scripture says, "Whoever believes on Him will not be put to shame." For there is no distinction between Jew and Greek, for the same Lord over all is rich to all who call upon Him. For "whoever calls on the name of the Lord shall be saved"* (Rom. 10:9-13).

We simply need to hear and believe this good news and "call on the name of the Lord" in prayer to be saved from our sin.

This gospel is so simple to share. Many Christians have yet to dare to care enough to share their expression of this good news with others. Paul wrote, "For I am not ashamed of the gospel of Christ, for it is the power of God to salvation for everyone who believes" (Rom. 1:16). All of heaven rejoices when one believes the gospel message of the His blood shed for us on the cross and calls upon Him in prayer. We need to commit the following prayer to memory and be bold in our ministry to lead others to salvation in Jesus Christ.

> Father God, I declare that I believe that Jesus Christ is Your Son. I believe that He shed His blood so my sins might be forgiven. I believe in my heart that You raised Him from the dead. I acknowledge that Jesus is the only way to You and to receive Your eternal life. I now make Jesus my Savior and Lord. Every work of the devil is broken in my life. I understand that I will spend eternity in heaven and not hell when I die. I receive Your Spirit now for the new birth of my spirit. I am now a new creation, born again by my faith in You and Your Son. I further declare that I will serve Jesus and follow Him the rest of my life.

Reconciliation means that God has made peace with a fallen world through the blood shed by His only Son Jesus Christ. "As it is written: How beautiful are the feet of those who preach the gospel of peace, Who bring glad tidings of good things!" (Rom. 10:15). The gospel is about God making peace with the entire world through His Son's death, burial, and resurrection as the ultimate act of love.

I greatly rejoice with the privilege of standing behind a pulpit to teach God's people the Word by the inspiration of the Holy Spirit. It has also been rewarding to care for God's flock as a pastor in a local church. It's both a joy and delight to serve God and His people in the expressions of a pastor, teacher, and minister within the local church.

Yet as wonderful as these responsibilities are, nothing compares to when I have stood on an open-air crusade platform as part of an evangelistic team. It is marvelous to stand before masses of people in a dark part of the world who have come to hear the preaching of the glorious gospel. Nothing compares to witnessing hundreds and sometimes thousands believe the message of the glorious gospel for the first time and call upon Jesus Christ as their personal Savior. We can also know this joy as we dare to share this message one-on-one with someone outside our church walls.

We have been entrusted with our Lord's authoritative command to "Go into all the world and preach the gospel to every creature" (Mark 16:15). Every Christian has been assigned with this number one purpose in their expression of God's love to take His Great Commission to the world. Every church member enters their mission field when they walk out the church doors. There ought to be a large banner at every church exit that reads, "Dare 2 Care." Then we are on our way to making our purpose about His number one purpose of ministering His message of reconciliation to a lost world that needs to receive the One we have received. The Gospel message is not to be kept secret. It is good news to be shouted from the roof tops.

CHAPTER 7

Bear Whose Burdens?

The church that Deborah and I were attending was preparing to take a group to travel out-of-state for a helps ministry seminar. The Lord gently spoke "Galatians 6:2" to my heart before the trip. I wasn't immediately sure of the text for that particular verse. I opened my Bible to find the phrase, "Bear one another's burdens."

Shortly thereafter, my pastor asked if I would personally look after a particular man during the seminar. He was a new member of our church and expressed interest in wanting to go with us. But he was extremely overweight and had serious health issues. He had severe respiratory conditions due to his weight and a previous history of abusing drugs.

My pastor had me take him shopping for some new clothes for the trip. I shared a hotel room with him during the seminar to help with his sleeping respiratory equipment. It was even arranged to secure a cart to transport him from building to building. Afterward, my pastor personally thanked me for assisting him in my attempt to fulfill Galatians 6:2 to bear another person's burdens.

Paul admonished those who were spiritual are to bear the burdens of others,

Brethren, if a man is overtaken in any trespass, you who are spiritual restore such a one in a spirit of gentleness, considering yourself lest you also be tempted. Bear one another's burdens, and so fulfill the law of Christ (Gal. 6:1-2).

Paul also told the church at Rome,

We who are strong (in our convictions and of robust faith)

*ought to bear with the failings and the frailties and the tender
scruples (or weaknesses) of the weak. We ought to help carry the
doubts and qualms of others—and not to please ourselves*
(Rom. 15:1 Amp).

We are instructed to help bear and carry the burdens of those
who are weak. A sign of spiritual maturity is a sacrificial willingness to put others above pleasing ourselves.

We are to love them as we love ourselves. Jesus was asked,

*"Teacher, which is the great commandment in the law?"" Jesus
said to him, "You shall love the LORD your God with all your
heart, with all your soul, and with all your mind. This is the
first and great commandment. And the second is like it: You
shall love your neighbor as yourself. On these two commandments hang all the Law and the Prophets"* (Matt. 22:36-40).

Our attitude toward people will determine our altitude with
God. The Lord Himself said there is no other commandment
greater than these—to love your God with all your heart, soul, and
mind, and to love your neighbor as yourself. Some people love God
but have issues with one another. Beware of an attitude like the
teacher who said, "Teaching would be enjoyable if it weren't for the
students." We don't want to have a similar view as the one who
said, "I wouldn't mind ministry if it weren't for the people." People
are reason for the expression of our Lord's ministry to one another.

Relationships with others are our greatest treasures on earth.
Yet too many people chase the wrong priorities. I observed a message on a shirt that read, "Lust will leave you loveless. Money will
leave you comfortless. Power will leave you heartless. Drugs and
alcohol will leave you senseless."

The most important things in life are God and people—not
things. The Lord taught us to "seek first the kingdom of God and
His righteousness, and all these things shall be added to you"
(Matt. 6:33). As we put first things first—God and our fellow
man—the secondary things will be added by the Lord.

Our relationships can become our greatest legacy in this life. Our first priority is our relationship with the Father, Son, and Holy Spirit. Then our love for God will motivate our love and relationships with our fellow man.

As Jesus lay down His life for all, we are to likewise love one another by laying down our lives for others (John 15:12-13). It was God's love for the people of the world that motivated Him to give the gift of His Son. Jesus ministered by the power of the Holy Spirit to be a blessing to others as God was with Him as He "went about doing good" (Acts 10:38). The people were the expression for His priority, purpose, and plan for ministry.

Life of Giving

"If we walk in the light as He is in the light, we have fellowship with one another, and the blood of Jesus Christ His Son cleanses us from all sin" (1 John 1:7). Follow His example to discover that a life worth living is a life of giving. His abundant life is about giving and blessing others not just about receiving and being blessed. Find the real blessing in giving as the Lord taught, "It is more blessed to give than to receive" (Acts 20:35).

Consider what Paul wrote to the church at Corinth,

For as the body is one and has many members, but all the members of that one body, being many, are one body, so also is Christ. For by one spirit we were all baptized into one body — whether Jews or Greeks, whether slaves or free — and have all been made to drink into one spirit. For in fact the body is not one member but many. If the foot should say, "Because I am not a hand, I am not of the body," is it therefore not of the body? And if the ear should say, "Because I am not an eye, I am not of the body," is it therefore not of the body? If the whole body were an eye, where would be the hearing? If the whole were hearing, where would be the smelling? But now God has set the members, each one of them, in the body just as He pleased. And if

51

they were all one member, where would the body be? But now indeed there are many members, yet one body. And the eye cannot say to the hand, "I have no need of you"; nor again the head to the feet, "I have no need of you." No, much rather, those members of the body which seem to be weaker are necessary. And those members of the body which we think to be less honorable, on these we bestow greater honor; and our unpresentable parts have greater modesty, but our presentable parts have no need. But God composed the body, having given greater honor to that part which lacks it (1 Cor. 12:12-24).

The Bible compares the body of Christ to the physical body. The human body is a great example of how our relationships within the body of Christ ought to work. Every part of His body is important including the "weaker" parts that have burdens and need help from others. Even "those members of the body which we think to be less honorable" are precious to the Lord.

Each member of the body—whether weak or strong—has its own unique design and function. The body can survive with some body parts missing, but all body parts are useless and can't survive apart from the body. Every member of the church is a valued minister. When each individual member-minister finds their place and fills their role, the entire body is able to fully function as it was created to.

Every Christian Has a Function

As members of one body in Christ, every Christian has a function in the church.

For as we have many members in one body, but all the members do not have the same function, so we, being many, are one body in Christ, and individually members of one another. Having then gifts differing according to the grace that is given to us" (Rom. 12:4-6).

We are each like crucial pieces to a giant jigsaw puzzle, the puzzle of the body of Christ. Each individual piece is necessary to complete the total picture. Each piece needs to be assembled together to reveal the image of Christ formed and imprinted upon His entire body. There are too many pieces who are A.W.O.L. (Absent WithOut Leave). We are all to man our post and find our place as individual "members of one another."

Jesus has specific functions, roles, duties, and divine assignments of expression for every believer. We have orders from headquarters to be His reflection to one another as we share our gifts, talents, skills, resources, and abilities. All have a place in their local church to be fitly joined together shoulder-to-shoulder in support of each other. If we don't do our part individually, then the body of Christ will be lacking. The desire of each member of the church is to allow the Lord to use them to minister His expression to His body. This brings greater unity to a community within the body of Christ.

Our youngest son, Myles, was an active five-year-old showing off to me his newfound ability to hang onto a handrail at church. He declared to me, "Daddy, watch this. It's dangerous!" I asked, "Why are you doing it then?" He replied, "'Cause it's dangerous!" As a protective parent, I was close by to make sure that any of his "dangerous" choices wouldn't put him at risk of bodily injury.

The Lord has also put safeguards over us to make sure we don't fall prey to the enemy as we're instructed, "Be sober, be vigilant; because your adversary the devil walks about like a roaring lion, seeking whom he may devour" (1 Pet. 5:8).

The scriptures call us sheep of His flocks. As practically defenseless, sheep need a shepherd to help protect them from any dangers. Jesus is called our Great and Chief Shepherd (Heb. 13:20; 1 Pet. 5:4). Our Shepherd Jesus gives us under-shepherd pastors to watch over us. Individual sheep that are separated from the herd make for easier prey to predators. Like such a predator, Satan seeks "whom he may devour." It spells disaster for a believer to be separated from the rest of their flock.

An isolated saint is like a fort without walls that are exposed to the deceptive attacks from the enemy if they aren't in the midst of their own company. We find protection in numbers as herd of animals, schools of fish or flocks of birds do in nature. Remember, it's the banana separated from the bunch that gets peeled. No Christian man or woman should be an island to themselves as "none of us lives to himself" (Rom. 14:7).

The founding fathers of the United States of America declared at the signing of the Declaration of Independence, "We must all hang together, else we shall hang separately." God has instructed us to hang together in an inspired, authentic community of like faith believers.

One can choose to be a limited island to their self or tap into a continent of wealth by staying plugged into His body through our local church. We all need the expressions of ministry of other Christian people, and they need our expression of ministry. By building bridges to one another instead of erecting silos that separate, we accept our corporate ministerial role to become a contributing member to what God is doing now in the body of Christ.

For example, sick members are to call for the elders of the church for prayer.

Is anyone among you sick? Let him call for the elders of the church, and let them pray over him, anointing him with oil in the name of the Lord. And the prayer of faith will save the sick, and the Lord will raise him up. And if he has committed sins, he will be forgiven. Confess your trespasses to one another, and pray for one another, that you may be healed (Jam. 5:14-16).

If sin has opened the door for those burdened with sickness, the elders are to pray for their restoration and forgiveness. Working together, church leadership is to be accessible to "pray for one another" in assisting the sick, the weak and the burdened.

Therefore, it is vital for each member to find their place of ful-fillment in Christian expression within their local church assembly to give to others by the gift of the indwelling Holy Spirit. What God gives to us, He wants to get though us for the benefit of others. We all need each other.

This requires a team effort where everyone provides their share. I know coaches who have taken the acronym T.E.A.M. to mean Together Each Achieving More. By working together, we also become another kind of T.E.A.M.—Together Expressing A Ministry. There are no stars on this team except the Father, Son, and Holy Spirit. Our roles are discovered on this team when we make contributions to help others in need.

We are many members of one another as part of the body of Christ. When we minister to His body, we are ministering to Him. When I minister to my wife's body with a back rub or a foot mas-sage, I am ministering to the real Deborah that I love inside the body. My love for her is demonstrated with how I touch her body. Jesus cannot be physically touched by us here on earth. However, we can express our love for Him and touch Him by ministering to His body, the church.

Plugged in to God's church, ordinary people can live extraordi-nary lives by their connection with their group and make a differ-ence. Throughout history, individuals have united for a specific goal and achieved the impossible. When individuals work together to achieve a common goal, there is power available to the group that wasn't available to the individual. The whole is indeed greater than the sum of the individual parts. When it comes to any team or group partnership, each committed individual has their role to play. And when each person finds his or her place, the whole team is stronger and benefits from it.

There seems at first to be a contradiction when Paul writes to the church at Galatia to "bear one another's burdens" and then three verses later declares, "For each one shall bear his own load"

(Gal. 6:2-5). Why bear others' burdens if they are to bear their own load? We are to bear the burdens of the weak but the time will come for the weak to mature and eventually bear their own loads. Everyone needs to grow spiritually so that they can bear their own load and then help other weaker members with their burdens.

It should be the goal of every Christian to become that person others can turn to in a time of crisis. Be there for the burdened without becoming a permanent crutch for them. The goal is to help them so they can later help others as productive leaders in their local church assembly.

The greatest gift that the Lord gave to us was Himself. The greatest gift that we can give Him in return is ourselves. We are giving ourselves to Jesus who is the Head of the church when we give ourselves to the church which is His body. As we invest ourselves into others and bear their burdens for His sake, we will each find His plan of ministry for us within the church. The primary ministry of every Christian is to give to become a reflection of God's love to one another. We will discover the fulfillment of this ministry when we please the Master by demonstrating our love for Him as we give our gift of expression to each other.

CHAPTER 8

Receive Our Gift

When he first heard about Jesus and His home region, Nathanael seems to have said in a sarcastic tone, "Can anything good come out of Nazareth?" (John 1:46). Nazareth must have been an out-of-the-way place similar to my home state of Kansas. Some people from the east or west coast may likewise say, "Can anything good come out of Kansas?" Being a native of Kansas, I may be viewed by some as being geographically impaired.

There are certain aspects of life in the flatlands of the Midwest that are quite unique. For example, one might be from rural Kansas if their closest neighbor is more than a mile away, and they can still see their neighbor's house from their front porch. One might be from the Sunflower State if a traffic jam involves two cars staring each other down at a four-way stop, each determined to be the most polite and let the other go first. Our idea of traffic congestion is when ten cars have to wait to pass a combine on the highway.

One might be from Kansas when they have switched from heat to air conditioning on the same day. Most rural Kansans probably know of neighbors who installed security lights on their house and garage and then left both unlocked. Almost everyone from Kansas knows that a tornado warning siren is our signal to go out in the yard and look for a funnel. And one is definitely from Kansas if they have been asked, "Where is Toto?" more than once.

As a young boy growing up in Midway USA, I can remember the excitement of opening gifts on Christmas morning. I would not leave any gift unopened even if it was just socks and underwear. As Christian believers, we should be determined to receive

57

and open every gift from the Lord. Jesus paid the supreme price by His sufferings on the cross to provide all of the glory of heaven's riches for us.

There are special gifts that God places in local churches for our benefit. We are in the wrong place if we aren't attending the local church that God wants each of us to attend. Such an impairment will cause us to miss the opportunity to open a special gift given to us by Jesus Christ Himself. When one is not attending church or attending the wrong church, they could be called directionally dysfunctional. They are missing their opportunity to receive and open the gift of a pastor given to them by God. It is written,

> *But to each one of us grace was given according to the measure of Christ's gift. Therefore He says: "When He ascended on high, He led captivity captive, And gave gifts to men..." And He Himself gave some to be apostles, some prophets, some evangelists, and some pastors and teachers, for the equipping of the saints for the work of ministry, for the edifying of the body of Christ, till we all come to the unity of the faith and of the knowledge of the Son of God, to a perfect man, to the measure of the stature of the fullness of Christ; that we should no longer be children, tossed to and fro and carried about with every wind of doctrine, by the trickery of men, in the cunning craftiness of deceitful plotting, but, speaking the truth in love, may grow up in all things into Him who is the head—Christ—from whom the whole body, joined and knit together by what every joint supplies, according to the effective working by which every part does its share, causes growth of the body for the edifying of itself in love* (Eph. 4:7-8, 11-16).

Our Lord gave gifts to men, including the gifts of pastors and teachers. He gave these gifts to some as an appointment, function, grace, or office. These persons then become gifts given to all the saints for the edifying of the body of Christ. Our pastor is a gift that Jesus gave to us through our local church.

The Work of the Ministry

There are two interpretations of verse 12 "for the equipping of the saints for the work of ministry, for the edifying of the body of Christ." The first view gives a distorted picture of the role of the pastor. In this inaccurate view, the pastor has a three-fold responsibility to equip the saints, to do the work of the ministry, and to edify the body of Christ. In other words, the pastor does all the giving in the work of ministry while the congregation does all the receiving.

The people watch as their gift—the minister—plays out the role of a celebrity athlete. The pastor becomes like their favorite football player. They come into the sanctuary stadium and pay the admission with their offerings. They passively sit in the stands (the pews) and watch their star on the playing field (the altar). They look entirely to the pulpit for big pass completions (and any fumbles) with more than sufficient after-service, post-game analysis.

These spectators (the congregation) buy into a concept similar to the television disclaimer warnings, "These are professionals; don't try this at home." From this perspective, the pastor is the active minister while the saints in the congregation are totally passive.

On the other hand, the correct way to properly view the gift of a pastor is to understand that he is a gift to equip the saints in order that *every believer* can do the work of the ministry. Every member of the body of Christ is to be a participating minister. We are all ministers who have these gifts to equip us all for the work of the ministry. A pastor is to equip their congregation for their personal ministry and the result is that the whole church becomes edified.

A pastor is not *the only* player but *a fellow* player who also serves like a coach. He coaches and equips the whole team to be players in the game of ministry. The church sanctuary becomes like a locker room for weekly pre-game speeches. When the service is over, the actual game is just starting. As a true outreach, they become a church without walls where every Christian has a ministry within and without the body of Christ. Every member is then a fruitful minister as a reflection of Jesus to the world and to the church.

The Pastor

In the past few decades, much of the church has experienced a rediscovery of the importance of the role of the pastor as an equipper. If the church is to function as God intended, the church is to be obedient to the command of Christ to "make disciples of all the nations" (Matt. 28:19). The pastor's priority is the equipping ministry of preparing saints *for works of service*. Everyone is a minister whether in an equipping lead ministry or a member of the congregation in a supportive ministry. A proper grasp of the respective roles in church is when the pastor fulfills his role as equipper and the saints fulfill their place as fellow ministers.

A pastor is a gift from the Lord Jesus that some saints unfortunately haven't fully received. Without this equipping gift, they will risk remaining as a spiritual child who can be "tossed to and fro and carried about with every wind of doctrine." When they fully receive this gift, they then will come to "the measure of the stature of the fullness of Christ" and "grow up in all things." Without their gifts, they will not fully mature and be equipped to be about His purpose and plans in bringing their supply to "come to the unity of the faith" (Eph. 4:13-15).

Some may argue that since the word "pastor" is found only one time in the New Testament, it denotes less significance for this particular gift. However, the word pastor in its varying forms—overseer, bishop, shepherd, and elder—is used many times throughout the epistles written to the church. It is accurate to say that bishop, overseer, shepherd, pastor, and elder all describe the pastoral office and leadership necessary in the local church. God appoints a pastor to act as an under-shepherd to oversee His church for the benefit of the saints.

The Lord promises His people that He will set up pastors over them.

But I will gather the remnant of My flock out of all countries where I have driven them, and bring them back to their folds; and they shall be fruitful and increase. I will set up shepherds over them who will feed them; and they shall fear no more, nor be dismayed, nor shall they be lacking, says the LORD (Jer. 23:3-4).

As a shepherd cares for a flock of sheep, a pastor is a feeder who provides spiritual nourishment to the ones whom the Lord has set under them so that God's people shall be fruitful and increase. He cares and feeds them so they will multiply, increase, and mature to fullness in Him.

The way Ephesians 4:11 groups pastors and teachers together seems to indicate that the office of a pastor and teacher can function together. Paul said a bishop (or a pastor) ought to be "apt to teach" (1 Tim. 3:2 KJV). They are apt to teach sound biblical doctrine instead of doctrinal tangents or extreme teachings. Those who fill the office of pastor-teacher teach the Word not by a natural ability but by the divine ability of the Holy Spirit. Teachers rightly divide the word of truth and skillfully train believers in true scriptural doctrine (2 Tim. 2:15).

It is a great responsibility to teach others as James wrote, "My brethren, let not many of you become teachers, knowing that we shall receive a stricter judgment" (Jam. 3:1). The Amplified Bible makes this accountability even more clear, "We (teachers) will be judged by a higher standard and with greater severity (than other people). Thus we assume the greater accountability and the more condemnation." With the greater responsibility, though, come the greater rewards.

At a leader's conference, Paul told the pastors present that the Holy Spirit Himself "has made you overseers, to shepherd in the church of God" (Acts 20:28). It is God who has "set some in the church" to govern and oversee the well-being of His people (1 Corinthians 12:28 KJV). These gifts of apostle, prophet, evangelist, pastor, and teacher have been classified as the five-fold ministry or the pulpit ministry. No person calls themselves into any of these five ministries. These gifts are a divine call made by God alone. There is a supernatural equipping bestowed upon a person who stands in any of these ministry offices. His love for His sheep motivated the Chief Shepherd to give the gift of pastor appointed to oversee His local flocks.

When Jesus "saw the multitudes, He was moved with compassion" for the "weary and scattered" multitudes as sheep having no shepherd (Matthew 9:36). Jesus is the Chief Shepherd and pastors are His designated shepherds for all of His flock. The Great Shepherd appoints under-shepherds as leaders after His own heart to be His gifts to be received by His sheep.

His under-shepherds are to govern, take care of, and watch over the sheep in the local church body of believers. No one else has authority over that shepherd's flock. The pastor is entrusted by God with the authority and responsibility with the oversight of their flock.

And we urge you, brethren, to recognize those who labor among you, and are over you in the Lord and admonish you, and to esteem them very highly in love for their work's sake. Be at peace among yourselves (1 Thess. 5:12-13).

We should esteem those which labor and are over us in the Lord. Our overseers are gifts to us from Jesus Himself to be received honorably in appreciation and high esteem.

Faith Is Necessary

It takes faith in order to receive the leader-ministers whom God has set in the local church. There must be faith on the lead minister's part as well as on the part of the supportive member ministers being ministered to. Walking by faith in this area requires learning to honor the people whom God has chosen to stand in this leadership office of ministry. A congregation that lightly esteems the pastor who labors among them will receive only a limited amount from the gift in their midst.

As a pastor, I have been received different ways by different people. I have purposed to be real and transparent as a personable leader to our congregation. I have found that more people appreciate my genuineness in finding out that I am human and have to deal with the same challenges of everyday life. It will take some maturity on the part of the flock to realize that, away from the pulpit, their shepherd is just as human as anyone else. We need to guard that we don't under-esteem those with whom we have become familiar.

Over-familiarity with the normalness of a pastor can be a hindrance to some members of a congregation. There are some who can't handle knowing their leader according to the flesh. "Therefore, from now on, we regard no one according to the flesh" (2 Cor. 5:16). Unfortunately, few people are mature enough spiritually to get to know a pastor in a close way and still receive the office in which they stand.

Even our Lord dealt with dishonor in His earthly ministry.

But Jesus said to them, "A prophet is not without honor except in his own country, among his own relatives, and in his own house." Now He could do no mighty work there, except that He laid His hands on a few sick people and healed them. And He marveled because of their unbelief (Mark 6:4-6).

Jesus went back to His hometown to minister where they wouldn't receive or honor Him. They knew Jesus as Mary's boy who grew up in the neighborhood. Their lack of honor toward Him caused unbelief on their part. The people of Nazareth knew Jesus after the flesh and would not receive Him as the Messiah and therefore, He "could there do no mighty work there." Guard against this happening in wrong attitudes toward our leadership gifts within our church staff.

It is best to maintain accountable relationships with our spiritual overseer and their leadership team within our local church. As a navigational GPS device assists those with a tendency for directional dysfunction, the Holy Spirit will guide us to the church where we can open His gift of pastor. Our local church with our gift from God will provide a place of rest, a place for protection, a place to be fed, and a place for our body ministry of expression. Like Dorothy from Kansas in the Wizard of Oz, we will then be able to say, "There is no place like home!"

CHAPTER 9

Serve Our Servant

I grew up as an obnoxious Jayhawk fan born in Lawrence, the home of the University of Kansas. During my sophomore year, I wore a KU shirt almost every day to high school. I attended rural schools in small agricultural communities outside of Topeka where the majority of my classmates were Kansas State University fanatics. We thrived on ribbing one another when our team won in basketball or football.

Rex is my best friend from junior college and a board member of our ministry. We both became radical for Jesus during our sophomore year in college. After we graduated from Butler Community College, he transferred to run track as a walk-on at his beloved Kansas State University. Rex tells all who will listen that he roots for two teams—K-State and whoever is playing KU.

During one Sunday sermon, I used Rex's passion as an object lesson. No one else but God knew what I was about to do. I had only asked Chuck (our "Mr. Sound Man" in the sound booth) to have a camera ready for something that would happen later in the service.

My sermon text was 1 Corinthians 9:22 where Paul stated, "I have become all things to all men, that I might by all means save some." I gave a personal example that I, as a KU Jayhawk, could become all things (even a K-State Wildcat) to save some Wildcats. I took off my tie and unbuttoned my dress shirt to reveal a K-State t-shirt underneath.

I then put Rex on the spot and asked him to come forward to "lay down his life" for his pastor and friend. Rex reluctantly walked forward to the pulpit area as I gave him a KU hat to put on to demonstrate that he, as a Wildcat, could become all things (even a Jayhawk) to save some Jayhawks.

It wasn't easy, but he was a good sport and honored my request with a true servant's heart. The funniest part was when he went back to his seat. The Jayhawk hat proved too much as he failed to sit in his previous seat by his wife, Karen. He instead mistakenly sat in Chuck's vacated seat beside his wife, Anne. We all probably have never laughed harder in church together than we did that memorable Sunday morning.

Every believer is called to be a minister with a ministry to serve others in true Christian expression. "As each one has received a gift, minister it to one another, as good stewards of the manifold grace of God" (1 Pet. 4:10). Every Christian has within them the gift of the Holy Spirit. This inward gift empowers us all to minister as good stewards to one another. We are ministers equipped with His Spirit to give God's grace to others within the church and take the salvation gospel to the world. All believers have received the ministry of reconciliation (2 Cor. 5:18-20) as His ambassadors who are to share His word of reconciliation. Our supply and ministry will cause the growth of the body of Christ.

We are all to do our share by being strategically connected members of His church. As we find our role, we can play a crucial part in the spiritual growth of those around us. This is our part of serving an important function in the local body of believers in which He places us.

Our local church and our role in it are God's choices not ours. In a proper family setting, each member has his own particular function. No one is more important than another, and success is only achieved when everyone works together toward a common purpose.

Most people think of a minister as the pastor or a preacher. In the Bible, a Greek word used for minister literally means "an under rower on a boat." The general idea implied is someone who is a servant, helper, or assistant with the predominant idea of subordination. Unfortunately, too many Christians are known for their insubordination instead of subordination. Subordination means to be at the disposal of others to meet their needs and carry out their wishes. That is what true ministry is about. The more subordinated an individual serves as that under rower to Jesus and His body, the higher their position of greatness in the eyes of God.

Our Lord had to deal with some turmoil and competition among His disciples as to whom among them would have the greatest authority in His kingdom.

> *Then the mother of Zebedee's sons came to Him with her sons, kneeling down and asking something from Him. And He said to her, "What do you wish?" She said to Him, "Grant that these two sons of mine may sit, one on Your right hand and the other on the left, in Your kingdom." And when the ten heard it, they were greatly displeased with the two brothers. But Jesus called them to Himself and said, "You know that the rulers of the Gentiles lord it over them, and those who are great exercise authority over them. Yet it shall not be so among you: but whoever desires to become great among you, let him be your servant. And whoever desires to be first among you, let him be your slave—just as the Son of Man did not come to be served, but to serve, and give His life a ransom for many"* (Matt. 20:20-21,24-28).

The Lord taught them "whoever desires to become great among you, let him be your slave." Jesus gave His example as He "did not come to be served, but to serve, and give His life a ransom for many." He later proclaimed, "But he who is greatest among you shall be your servant. And whoever exalts himself will be humbled, and he who humbles himself will be exalted" (Matt. 23:11-12). From the Lord's perspective, expressions of Christian ministry are not so much about position, preaching, and power as they are primarily exhibiting the heart of a serving servant.

Jesus humbled Himself and took the form of a bondservant and became obedient to His Father's will.

Let this mind be in you which was also in Christ Jesus, who, being in the form of God, did not consider it robbery to be equal with God, but made Himself of no reputation, taking the form of a bondservant, and coming in the likeness of men. And being found in appearance as a man, He humbled Himself and became obedient to the point of death, even the death of the cross (Phil. 2:5-8).

A supporting minister's position may be secondary in nature, but it's not an inferior position. Jesus took upon Himself a secondary role by becoming a servant to the Father. However, He was not inferior to the Father. On a personal level, He was equal to the Father. On a functional level, He served by giving up His own will and desire in order to do His Father's will and desire.

Jesus yielded Himself in total obedience to the Father's will and plan. At Gethsemane in agony and sweating drops of blood, He prayed, "Father, if it is Your will, take this cup away from Me; nevertheless not My will, but Yours, be done" (Luke 22:42-44). A servant's attitude is found in His repeated declaration, "Not my will, but Yours, be done."

Like a servant, Jesus washed the disciple's feet. We are to follow our Lord's example by humbling ourselves as bondservants.

Likewise you younger people, submit yourselves to your elders. Yes, all of you be submissive to one another, and be clothed with humility, for "God resists the proud, But gives grace to the humble." Therefore humble yourselves under the mighty hand of God, that He may exalt you in due time (1 Pet. 5:5-6).

God is looking for ministers with servant's hearts who will submit to their elders and be submissive to one another while clothed with His reflections of humility. It's pride to not take on the mantle of a true servant. God will resist the proud but He gives grace to the humble servant. We will be exalted and be great in His kingdom when we become a servant to Him and others as we minister His love. It is written, "Through love serve one another" (Gal. 5:13).

We need to choose to commit to the ministry of serving one another. Every Christian is called to the ministry of being a servant expression to others. The rewards in His kingdom are great for those who prove themselves to God and pass the servant's test. God will approve those who are candidates for future promotions into greater ministry opportunities. Because the Lord can trust those who are faithful in their service to others, He will promote them.

Preparation for Leadership

A leadership position is about serving not being served. God prepares leaders for greater levels of service as they first serve other leaders. Jesus said, "And if you have not been faithful in what is another man's, who will give you what is your own?" (Luke 16:12). God may be using our time spent to serve leadership as a means of preparing for future assignments.

Future leaders in ministry were first prepared in supportive ministry by serving the servant of God. Examples of special dream teams are found in the Bible who God put together as companions for His glory. "So the LORD spoke to Moses face to face, as a man speaks to his friend. And he would return to the camp, but his servant Joshua the son of Nun, a young man, did not depart from the tabernacle" (Exodus 33:11).

Though Moses spoke to God face to face, Joshua (Moses' faithful servant and assistant) did not depart from the tabernacle, remaining in God's glory in preparation for future promotion.

Joshua faithfully served God's leader for more than 40 years until Moses laid hands on him to be his successor (Deut. 34:9). God prepared Joshua for a leadership position while he served another leader. Joshua served as the personal assistant to Moses and eventually became a strong leader himself. Many others also served Moses including Aaron, Hur, Caleb, Miriam, and the elders.

In another Bible example of preparation for leadership service, Elisha also proved faithful to serve a leader in ministry before God put him into his own leadership position. Like Moses, Elijah also had a close relationship with an assistant servant who later was promoted to do great exploits for God. With no hesitation, Elisha literally burned all his bridges behind by burning his oxen to follow Elijah and "became his servant" (1 Kings 19:21). Various translations say that Elisha became Elijah's disciple, attendant, and assistant.

Elisha was known as the prophet's servant "who poured water on the hands of Elijah" (2 Kings 3:11). He was humble enough to serve for years as a human faucet. Elisha faithfully served God by serving a servant of God before receiving his ministry as the successor to the prophet (2 Kings 2:1-15). Church historians vary whether Elisha served Elijah for somewhere between seven to twenty-five years before he received a double portion of his predecessor's mantle.

Elijah had another servant before Elisha was chosen. He was the servant whom Elijah sent seven times to look toward the sea for rain while he prayed to end the drought. That servant didn't stick like Elisha and remained behind when Elijah ran from Jezebel (1 Kings 19:3). On the other hand, despite Elijah's insistence for Elisha to repeatedly stay behind, he refused to leave his side as they traveled to Gilgal, Bethel, Jericho, and Jordan. Elisha was determined to stay close and serve his mentor while the other sons of the prophets remained afar off.

When considering what the apostles accomplished in the book of Acts, it's easy to forget that they spent more than three years first serving the Minister. They manned the boat in the middle of the night while Jesus slept on a pillow. They went for food while Jesus rested at the well in Samaria. They went for the donkey and set up the upper room. As Jesus multiplied the loaves and fishes, they organized the people in groups of fifty and collected the left-over loaves.

Faithfulness in serving within another leader's ministry must be shown before God will trust one to be faithful in their future leadership ministry. These disciples served the Lord as they pre-pared for their future ministries. They were in effect in training by serving another minister.

Seven men were chosen to minister by serving the apostles and the people in the church by serving bread. This allowed the leader-ship of the church at Jerusalem to focus their time on prayer and the word.

> *Therefore, brethren, seek out from among you seven men of good reputation, full of the Holy Spirit and wisdom, whom we may appoint over this business; but we will give ourselves continu-ally to prayer and to the ministry of the word. And the saying pleased the whole multitude. And they chose Stephen, a man full of faith and the Holy Spirit, and Philip, Prochorus, Nicanor, Timon, Parmenas, and Nicolas, a proselyte from Antioch, whom they set before the apostles; and when they had prayed, they laid hands on them* (Acts 6:3-6).

After first volunteering to wait tables to serve the apostles and the church in Jerusalem, Stephen and Philip went on to operate mightily in the power of God. "Stephen, full of faith and power, did great wonders and signs among the people (Acts 6:8). "Then Philip went down to the city of Samaria and preached Christ to them. And the multitudes with one accord heeded the things spoken by Philip, hearing and seeing the miracles which he did" (Acts 8:5-6).

Stephen could have rejected the menial tasks of waiting on tables if he said, "This is beneath me. I only do great wonders and signs." Philip could have balked if he said, "I'm an evangelist not a waiter." But they never did. Instead, they served the people.

A case can be made that they served first as a prerequisite to preparation for further opportunities in ministry. The mantle of true humility to first serve as a supportive minister will be needed when one senses a call to a future leadership position. In the kingdom of God, we will only be as effective a leader as we are first a follower. Even when a promotion to leadership comes, a leader still remains a true servant to others.

It's clear from the book of Acts that two of the seven bread servers were used in other powerful expressions of ministry. The other five bread servers apparently found their permanent place in supportive ministerial positions to the apostles and their church. Some will move on to a promotion in leadership while others will remain in a specific supportive position in ministry on a permanent basis. The key is to seek God to know your place and then faithfully serve in your role within the church.

"Remember those who rule over you, who have spoken the word of God to you, whose faith follow, considering the outcome of their conduct" (Hebrews 13:7). The majority of Christians are to serve in a supportive role in their church ministry as they remember, honor, and serve the servant whom God has placed over them. Our divine assignment is to continue to serve our servant leader as they serve us in serving the Lord together.

There is a positive influence by association. We learn about ministry while serving those who rule over us. We shouldn't stand alone but instead ask God to bring to us our divine connections who are filled with the strength of the Word and the Spirit. As we serve one another and remain hooked up with those who know and understand us personally, they will speak scripturally into our life and ministry. Our spiritual relationships will inspire us to rise to new heights in God. Their influence provides an environment that causes the seeds of our spiritual endowments to sprout and grow.

Our devotion to the service of the saints is an important element in our Christian expression. "I beseech you, brethren, (ye know the house of Stephanas, that it is the firstfruits of Achaia, and that they have addicted themselves to the ministry of the saints)" (1 Cor. 16:15 KJV). We need to be like the house of Stephanas by having an addiction to the ministry of the saints. We will be honored and rewarded in heaven when we make ourselves the servants of the saints.

Skilled servant work is the mark of fully mature adults who are truly like Christ as fully alive Christians. "He handed out gifts of apostle, prophet, evangelist, and pastor-teacher to train Christians in skilled servant work, working within Christ's body, the church, until we're all moving rhythmically and easily with each other, efficient and graceful in response to God's son, fully mature adults, fully developed within and without, full alive like Christ" (Eph. 4:11-13 Message). As skilled servants, we are to move rhythmically and easily with each other, working within our church.

The maturity of our personal reflection of Christ is measured by our expressions of skilled servant work motivated to bless others. We should come to church primarily to give not to receive. The heart of a servant is not to come to church to be solely ministered to but rather come with the commitment to minister to others. We become fully alive as we minister to the Lord and His people from a servant's heart of humility and sincerity. We serve the Lord by exhibiting His example when He served in His earthly ministry. As true servants, we are available to wash one another's feet and, if called upon, even wear our pastor-friend's KU Jayhawk hat. We serve our servants as leaders and supportive ministers, all serving one another skillfully as expressions in the Lord.

CHAPTER 10

"We Want Fred!"

I was always one of the smallest children in my school classes until I experienced a growth spurt my sophomore year in high school. I had tried out for nearly every sport in our rural community school but had limited early success due to my small stature. I eventually realized that my smaller frame was better suited for distance running than for the power-oriented team sports.

I can relate to the story of a skinny kid also named Fred who tried out for his junior high basketball team. Fred practiced hard but due to lack of talent, he spent most of his time on the end of the bench. His only playing time was the garbage minutes when the coach emptied the bench to let everyone play after the outcome of the game had already been determined.

One game, the boy's family decided to start chanting, "We want Fred! We want Fred!" Their hope was to influence the coach into making a substitution. Fred got even more embarrassed as his family continued to shout even louder. After several minutes of this, the coach called Fred over to his seat. His family then started to cheer more wildly in anticipation of Fred's entrance into the game.

Fred responded in the affirmative when his coach asked if he had heard his family in the stands yelling, "We want Fred!" The coach then said, "Well, go up there and see what they want."

The unfortunate reality in life is that we don't always get what we want. Waiting for what we want can be difficult when we don't get what we want when we want it. What we want is not always what we need. What we think we want isn't always in our best interest when we aren't prepared and ready yet.

Our oldest son, Kyle, was seven years old when he told me, "I'm going to be bigger just like you some day. In maybe, two weeks!" As his father, I knew that he would be bigger like me someday, but it was going to take much longer than his projected timeline.

We likewise can lack objectivity with unrealistic expectations for early ministerial promotions. Rest assured that our heavenly Father does know best. His kingdom is established on progressive maturity in full preparation for the right timing in promotion for successful ministry.

David's Preparation

As a 17-year-old youth, David was anointed by Samuel to be Saul's replacement as king of Israel but did not become king until he was 30 years of age. God continued to prepare his heart through years of progression in different stages of life and ministry. He began with a shepherd's lifestyle. David was faithful to take care of his father's house by tending the sheep in a field far away from the eyes of man. Yet God knew David's heart and eventually promoted him to be king of Israel after first being faithful as a sheep herder. David privately killed the lion and bear that threatened his father's sheep before the crowds witnessed his slaying of the giant.

David learned that there are no great victories without great battles. He developed personally both as a warrior and a worshipper. David became a serving armor bearer for King Saul and later was made captain over 1,000 troops. Despite his faithful service, Saul twice tried to pin him against the wall with his spear. David then had to flee for his life as Saul sought to end his life.

Samuel had prophesied over David that he would be the next king of Israel. Before long, those whom he was supposed to rule over were seeking to kill him. It looked as if the opposite of what Samuel had prophesied was coming to pass. Because of his integrity, David twice refused to kill the man who sought to have him murdered. He trusted God to establish him in his ordained position and wouldn't harm God's anointed. David became a stranger in a foreign land. It took 24 years of preparation after Samuel's anointing for David to finally become the actual king of all Israel.

Being Faithful

The majority of believers never come close to moving into the fullness of their ministry because they are unfaithful in the little that God has given them to do. God can't increase ministerial opportunities for someone who is not faithful to what God has already told them to do. Faithfulness is demonstrated by a willingness to joyfully serve with the most menial of assignments.

In climbing a ladder, no one starts out on the top rung. They begin on the bottom rung and climb up. Lynda, our dear friend and faithful assistant pastor, once floored a previous pastor with her request that she be allowed to clean the church's restrooms and toilets. Her heart was to serve even in the most humbling of duties.

Her faithfulness brought rapid promotion as she was soon the secretary of that church. She has exemplified a servant's heart as the most faithful member of our church with a willingness to do whatever asked of her. Even as the associate pastor of our church, she will still clean the restrooms without any hesitation.

There is a biblical principle that all aspiring ministers will learn concerning humble beginnings, "For who has despised the day of small things?" (Zech. 4:10). Ministries begin in an embryo stage and are developed with faithfulness. God won't use or promote the unfaithful.

A minister related to his humorous and humbling start in paying his dues in ministry before God's promotions came. He decided to visit a pastor in his town, hoping for an opportunity to preach. The pastor invited him to commit to prayer and other altar work. At first, he turned to walk away when the Lord spoke to his heart to tell the pastor he would do anything he was asked to do. He was insulted when the pastor invited him to take the vacant custodial position and clean the church. He told the pastor that he was called to preach and not be a janitor. After some sleepless nights, he returned to the church to become the new janitor.

After a period of faithfulness in his new position, he was asked to teach Sunday school. After his initial elation, he found out he would be teaching the toddlers to the three year olds. He was literally starting from the bottom up with changing diapers and such. Over time, he received subsequent promotions within the church from being the song leader to youth minister and then to associate pastor. When the existing pastor went to another church, he was asked to fill in as the new pastor. Finally, after not despising his day of small things, he was ready to be promoted to preach.

God's Timing

One of the most frustrating aspects of air travel is the inevitable delays. Those who think that travel sounds glamorous are obviously those who don't travel often. Frequent travelers know about flight delays at the gate, what it is to be stuck on the tarmac or put on a circling holding pattern in the air. Similar frustrations with God arise from our human perspective as He never seems to be in a hurry. By our standards, God always seems to take longer than we think he should.

"Let us not be weary in well doing: for in due season we shall reap, if we faint not" (Gal. 6:9 KJV). Given our hurried tendencies, guard against weariness that tests patience in remaining faithful in well doing. God will come through on time—His time. Our reaping in due season is promised. We are encouraged to "faint not" due to weariness during this process.

Impatience to force things or try to make it happen will not change God's divine timetable. God has His times and due seasons for each of us. Relax, be obedient, and patiently continue to walk in faithfulness with humility, meekness, and submission. His perfect timetable is necessary for fullness, maturity, and bringing everything together in proper order.

Our spiritual race in this life is certainly more of a marathon than a sprint. In 1980, I had qualified for the Olympic Trials marathon and was looking forward to a good result as I had been training 15 to 20 miles a day. A city newspaper sports reporter kept pressing me in an interview on how fast I hoped to run. I finally predicted a 2 hour 11 minute time for the 26.2 mile race.

At the trials, I ran with the leaders for the first 10 miles, then fell off the pace and jogged home to a disappointing finish. My embarrassing time was some 15 minutes slower than my quoted prediction printed in the front page of the sports section. However, four years later, I accomplished my predicted time. I had the race time right, but not when it would happen.

Abraham and Sarah tried to help God with their promised son. Abraham's impatience produced an Ishmael. The worst thing to do is think time is running out and try to help God by our own means. Be faithful to wait for the promised Isaac in God's perfect timing. Joseph's dream came true 22 years later.

Even Jesus had 30 years of life on earth in preparation before His three years of ministry—a ten-to-one ratio. In the meantime, He was faithfully about His Father's business even as a twelve-year-old. He continued to increase "in wisdom and stature, and in favor with God and men" until it was God's time for Him to begin His earthly ministry (Luke 2:49-52). Jesus acknowledged that the times and seasons are in the Father God's hands (Acts 1:7).

Few things in the kingdom of God are an instant deal or happen overnight. In our culture, quick service is taken for granted with our microwave meals and drive thru, fast food restaurants. The kingdom of God is not for the impatient or for those who want instant gratification. Be willing to wait patiently for God's timing.

Jesus taught,

The kingdom of God is as if a man should scatter seed on the ground, and should sleep by night and rise by day, and the seed should sprout and grow, he himself does not know how. For the earth yields crops by itself: first the blade, then the head, after that the full grain in the head. But when the grain ripens, immediately he puts in the sickle, because the harvest has come (Mark 4:26-29).

The seed of His Word must be planted, watered, cultivated, and weeded before the harvest comes. There are stages of development before grain ripens—the seed sprouting and growing—first the blade, then the head, and after the full grain in the head. Harvest will not precede germination, sprouting and growing as God works to accomplish His will for our lives.

In a parable, Jesus gave the illustration of seed finding good soil.

Not like the ones that fell among thorns are those who, when they have heard, go out and are choked with cares, riches, and pleasures of life, and bring no fruit to maturity. But the ones that fell on the good ground are those who, having heard the word with a noble and good heart, keep it and bear fruit with patience (Luke 8:14-15).

There are people who bring no fruit to maturity due to the pressures and the pleasures of life. The seed of God's Word did not find good soil in their hearts. Let's be like the ones with a noble and good heart, which are good ground in which to bear fruit.

It will be with patience that the seed of God's Word will produce lasting fruit. It takes both faith and patience to inherit the promises of God (Heb. 6:12). Patience is the power twin that works with faithfulness to inherit His promises. Faith opens the window of heaven while patience holds that window of promise open until His answer arrives.

The kingdom of patience is not compared to the man who demanded, "God, give me the gift of patience right now!" The Lord will "direct your hearts into the love of God and into the patience of Christ" (2 Thess. 3:5). Today's actions determine future tomorrows. We need to hear and do God's Word as seeds that are patiently planted in the good soil. These seeds grow, develop, and proceed to bring one maturity. These seedlings transform a believer from a spiritual babe to a responsible adult in Christ. Like a metamorphosis, they grow from carnal and flesh-ruled to mature and spirit-ruled. The maturation of the seed of His Word in the good ground of a heart will produce fruitful harvests of thirty-, sixty-, or a hundred-fold returns (Matt. 13:23).

The fruit of promotion comes from the seeds of faithfulness. It will require instant obedience in every area of life. In the meantime, let's relax and enjoy the journey. Let's be patient and let the Potter mold our character into His own as we become clearer reflections of His nature. We need to stay pliable in the Master's hands as we go from seedtime to harvest. It will require patience to allow God the time to lay a firm foundation while cooperating with the Him as His workmanship (Eph. 2:10). There is a maturation process before a seed grows to a ripened plant ready for the harvest.

We do not know much about our future. Jesus taught us to take no thought for tomorrow. Worrying about the future short-circuits our system's ability to live victoriously and carefree in the present. What God does choose to reveal to us about our future is so that we can properly prepare. We will not be ready for the future when it comes if we aren't preparing for it ahead of time.

Preparation time is not lost time. Most everyone wants to be promoted to their ultimate place in ministry, but not everyone wants to prepare for it. Look to the Lord for any promotion and not to man (Psalm 75:6-7). As we serve one another, it is actually He whom we are serving. Seek His promotion by doing it His way and not through man's ways. When the time comes for our promotion, let us not withdraw from it out of insecurity. As He has fully prepared us, we will be fully equipped. When Coach Holy Spirit calls us from the end of the bench, we'll be ready to make that key move in our ministry to one another.

His plan for us was always there from the foundation of time, but the proof of its fruition is evidenced by our submission to God's progressive training over a period of years. Our personal ministry will eventually be recognized by the rest of the body of Christ because of our years of proven faithfulness.

The divine seed of ministry is planted in the beginning by God and then incubated in the womb of prayer, obedience, and spiritual growth until God's appointed time for birthing. Even after the ministry of expression is birthed, there will be time before we reach the fullness of our potential in that ministry.

God's timing is just as important as God's plan. God declares "the end from the beginning" (Isaiah 46:10). He may show us a future finish line, and we may assume it will happen right away. In reality, He is showing our future so we can fully prepare for it.

God may be showing a scene from chapter nine in our life when we're still in chapter three. To run ahead of God and force things to happen will only bring confusion and disappointment. Many know the destination of their called ministry but not its perfect timing. Finding out the timing and how to get there is as important as our ministry itself.

We can rest assured that as we remain faithful to prepare, God will in His timing be faithful to open doors for more ministry opportunities. As I have been patient to prepare for promotion, the time will come when I'll hear the Father, Son, and Holy Spirit say, "We want Fred!" Then I will know when my due season has arrived, and it's His time for another opportunity and promotion in ministry.

CHAPTER 11

Well Done or Still Rare?

After my graduation from Butler Community College, I transferred to run on the cross country and track teams at Ft. Hays State University in western Kansas. My athletic ability progressed from an average high school runner to a collegiate national champion during my senior year when I won the three-mile run at the 1979 NAIA National Indoor Track and Field Championships.

While on a solo morning training run in a light snowstorm in the town that the locals fondly call "Hays, America," the Lord gave me two principles to follow as an aspiring Christian athlete. He gently spoke to my heart to give Him all the glory and to never be satisfied, so after college, I usually raced with "Jesus Is Lord" on the front of my singlet to glorify Him.

When we are satisfied, we sit on our laurels and no longer press on for greater accomplishments or hunger for more. The unsatisfied athletes are the motivated ones who will continue to make the sacrifices necessary and do the extra training to reach their potential and win future championships. We can either be satisfied with where we are and what we have accomplished in the past or we can press on with a desire for more. We should only be pleased with not settling for less than our best for Him.

I've often told Deborah that many people would like to experience her thrill of winning a race. Even if they had her talent, most of them would not be willing to pay the price she pays in training to achieve the fitness necessary to win at that level. They don't have the discipline to make a lifestyle of daily eight- to ten-mile training runs year round.

I won the 1984 Twin Cities Marathon in a world class time of 2:11:35. The first place prize money was $20,000. I commented to a friend about how the pay scale was pretty good at almost $10,000 an hour for that race day's efforts. He laughed about how that also translated to about a nickel a mile for all the training miles over the years that lead up to that particular race.

Faithfulness in What We Have Been Given

There is a finish line of glory awaiting those who faithfully serve the Lord and do His will while here on earth. Unfortunately, there will be those who want rewards in heaven but haven't lived a life with the faithfulness deserving of them.

Paul gave ministerial advice to Timothy, the pastor at the church in Ephesus.

You therefore, my son, be strong in the grace that is in Christ Jesus. And the things that you have heard from me among many witnesses, commit these to faithful men who will be able to teach others also (2 Tim. 2:1-2).

His instructions were to commit the teaching of others to faithful men. Education or great oratory skills were not listed as key prerequisites for selection. Faithfulness is the requirement that God is looking for before He commits to giving opportunities for service. In his first letter to Timothy, Paul stated that God had "committed to my trust ... the glorious gospel." Paul then added, "He counted me faithful, putting me into the ministry" (1 Tim. 1:11-13). God counted Paul as faithful before putting him into the ministry and trusting him with the preaching of the Gospel.

The faithful are dependable, reliable, and loyal. Their obligation is to defend and support while adhering to the performance of a duty. The faithful are true to their word and promises. They are never too big to do the small things or too small to do the big things. When it's called for, they are big enough to be rebuked and corrected by the Lord or His leadership. Those faithful to God and His church are known for longevity, commitment, positive attitude, and teamwork. Christians who continually apply these four traits will be ever breaking through instead of risking burnout.

Faithfulness is the necessary ingredient for excellence in any position in the local church. After a commitment has been made to be faithful, everything else revolves around that decision. The faithful are willing to go the extra mile. They are one of the first ones to arrive and one of the last ones to leave a church service. Pastors need reliable church members who can be counted on like the rising of the sun.

Faithfulness is not for the unstable who come when they want to, leave when they please and give financially when they feel like it. The faithful won't waste time to ponder where the Holy Spirit is leading them to go to church this week. They have found their place in His body and are sold out to faithful service at their post.

Pastors need faithful supportive ministers who support the ministries' vision prayerfully, physically, financially, and verbally. God delights in those who are faithful to their local church. These established Christians make up the backbone of a strong church.

God wants the faithful to grow and blossom where He plants them until He instructs them to go in another direction. Imagine a plant removing itself from its pot or constantly transplanting itself. How healthy could it be? When God plants someone in a church, the cry of their heart should be, "Lord, You can count on me to be faithful to serve You here until You give me further notice."

"A faithful man will abound with blessings" (Proverbs 28:20). Faithfulness precedes abounding blessings. Trustworthiness brings overwhelming blessings from heaven. God always rewards faithfulness. Even if it's not a pulpit ministry, all have a place for ministry of expression within His body. The ministry might be to usher, to teach the younger people, or to minister to a lost person at work.

The rewards come for faithfulness to what God has asked each of us to do and not just for the greater rewards of a high profile call. A faithful building maintenance person in the church will receive the same reward as a faithful pastor if that was God's plan for each of their lives.

We are to be faithful in our ministerial commitment to His work by using our gifts, talents, and abilities with honor and delight. Let's go the extra mile by giving more than what's expected. We should find a need at our local church and joyfully bring our supply to it in the behind-the-scenes activities. If we don't know where to begin, then let's consider what we do have and use it.

Pharaoh and the Egyptian army were marching toward the children of Israel. God told Moses to use the rod he had. He said, "Why do you cry to Me...? Lift up your rod and stretch your hand over the sea and divide it" (Exo. 14:10-16). A widow had only flour and oil but was obedient to the man of God's request. A young shepherd boy named David had only five stones and a sling shot but slew the giant. Jesus used a young boy's provision of some loaves and fishes. Dorca had needle and thread. Like Moses' rod, we will be faithful when we take what we have, throw it down in consecration, and pick it up in dedication.

A faithful person of their house of God will gladly do even the most menial of tasks for the good of their church and not seek credit from man. They have a joyful attitude and will take initiative to do what's necessary even before they are asked. They will cheerfully do the right thing in secret as unto the Lord in true service. They do not seek the praise from man because they know the Lord is their rewarder.

Paul commended several individuals in his writings for being faithful. They are each recorded in God's Word as faithful ministers and brothers. Paul mentioned Epaphras as "our dear fellow servant, who is a faithful minister of Christ" (Col. 1:7). He named Tychicus "a beloved brother, faithful minister, and fellow servant in the Lord" (Col. 4:7). He then sighted Onesimus as "a faithful and beloved brother" (Col. 4:9). The books of heaven will record whether we were one of the chosen stewards who are counted as faithful ministers and servants.

> *Let a man so consider us, as servants of Christ and stewards of the mysteries of God. Moreover it is required in stewards that one be found faithful* (1 Cor. 4:1-2).

As servants of Christ and stewards of the mysteries of God, it is required to be found faithful. Most all people are faithful, loyal and committed to something. Some are faithful to never miss certain television shows. Others are loyal to certain sporting events and teams. Yet others are committed to certain hobbies and lifestyles. All people are faithful, even if it's to the wrong things. It is wrong to make the temporal things of this life a priority over the eternal things. Faithfulness to the right things brings a great eternal inheritance.

Greater inheritance was promised to the two profitable servants,

> *Well done, good and faithful servant; you have been faithful over a few things, I will make you ruler over many things. Enter into the joy of your lord.*

The third unfaithful servant was called "wicked and lazy" by his lord who gave his inheritance to the faithful servants (Matt. 25:14-30).

When I hear the words "well done," I think of how I like my steak prepared—medium well. The good and faithful pair was "well done" in the sight of the Lord while the unfaithful servant was still rare. Greatness in God's kingdom is measured by how well his servants are faithful with what has been entrusted with them.

Our faithfulness over a few things in this life will bring us the reward of being "ruler over many things" now and in heaven. Some people want authority with no responsibility. They want opportunity with no accountability. God won't put an individual into a greater ministry responsibility if he has been unfaithful with lesser opportunities. The Lord can trust the faithful with authority over much when they have first taken responsibility over the little.

Team Effort

Throughout the ages, God has used faithful partners to work together in ministry. God said, "It is not good that man should be alone; I will make him a helper comparable to him" (Gen. 2:18) and created Eve to be a partner with Adam. Moses had a faithful team that included Joshua, Aaron, Hur, and the elders. Elijah had his servant Elisha. David had Jonathon and his mighty men. We see how Peter and John tag-teamed together with the healing of a lame man and five thousand men were saved as a result (Acts 3:1-4:4).

Paul teamed with Barnabas, Silas, Timothy, Luke, Titus, Mark, and others. Paul's ministry team was made up of both men and women who partnered with him for the sake of the Gospel. Though one person was recognized as the leader, God worked through a team effort.

Even Jesus, the Son of God, needed a team of faithful partners to help Him achieve all that God had asked Him to do. Jesus had the twelve disciples and later the seventy that He sent out in teams of two. It was a team effort as Jesus

> *went through every city and village, preaching and bringing the glad tidings of the kingdom of God. And the twelve were with Him, and certain women who had been healed of evil spirits and infirmities—Mary called Magdalene, out of whom had come seven demons, and Joanna the wife of Chuza, Herod's steward, and Susanna, and many others who provided for Him from their substance* (Luke 8:1-3).

There are divine connections and glorious associations in a

local church or ministry with God's intent to submit, honor, and love one another in one accord. We are stronger as a whole as we stand together. "If one prevail against him, two shall withstand him; and a threefold cord is not quickly broken" (Eccl. 4:12). There are no lone rangers in ministry. Even the Lone Ranger had Tonto as his faithful sidekick.

There is an old coaching cliché, "There is no 'I' in the word TEAM." The best sports teams are those that check their egos at the door and do what's in the best interest for the whole group. To be faithful in partnership, each unsatisfied member must yearn to put forth their best effort to fulfill their role for the good of the team effort. We need other faithful people for effective ministry.

Together with Him and with one another, His will for the local church will be accomplished through a team effort. It will take a well done not still rare ministerial effort by the collective group. No one is more important than another as success is only achieved when everyone works together toward the common purpose of glorifying Him. The result is synergetic because the cooperation of the group has a greater capacity for achievement. God is glorified when we are not just satisfied with a single individual effort but a greater corporate work in ministry that produces more fruit and increased reward in heaven.

CHAPTER 12

Duct Tape and Discipleship

When Myles was two-and-half years old, he was fascinated with all the tools we were using in a major construction project of our new church sanctuary. He wanted to be what he called, "one of the worker guys." Myles picked up a roll of duct tape and asked, "What's this?" Without waiting for my response and with all the passion of a true male, he quickly proclaimed loudly, "I like it!"

There are two things true of almost all men. The first is that we view duct tape as one of the greatest inventions in the known male world. Secondly, real men don't need instructions.

When Myles was older, he was playing a new video game with his brother. He told me, "It has instructions, but we don't need them." He was proof to the known fact that testosterone and instructions don't mix well.

One day I was mounting a ceiling fan in one of our boy's bedrooms. Many women will appreciate that this time I, as a man, was actually reading the ceiling fan instructions during installation. I was amused with the wording in these particular instructions which said to use "extreme patience" while taking "mandatory breaks." I concluded that men need extreme patience as much as they need direction and instruction.

The key ingredient to becoming a devoted disciple is willingness to follow our instruction book, the Bible. These instructions act as heavenly duct tape to hold it all together. In the Bible, the Lord has given us His instructions to follow, but how many of us (male and female) think we don't need them? When God gives us a commandment, we shouldn't treat it as a mere suggestion.

The church contains two kinds of believers—the whosoever-wills and the whosoever-will-nots. The whosoever-will-nots are the saints who don't bother to read or follow all His directions in the Book. The whosoever-wills are those who go on to become true disciples of Jesus as they continue to abide in His instructions.

There are traits that transform a believer into a true disciple as they commit to fully follow Him.

Great multitudes followed Him—from Galilee, and from Decapolis, Jerusalem, Judea, and beyond the Jordan. And seeing the multitudes, He went up on a mountain, and when He was seated His disciples came to Him (Matt. 4:25-5:1).

There are great multitudes of the whosoever-will-nots who will not follow the Lord all the way up the mountain.

His Disciples

There is a separation between the great multitudes of believers and those Jesus would call "My disciples." His disciples came up the mountain to Him while the multitudes stayed behind in the valley. The great multitudes are like the common believers who are content to remain valley sitters. In contrast, a disciple is a mountain climber. A conductor must turn his back to the crowd to lead the orchestra. The true core of the whosoever-wills will go wherever the Master goes. All are called to a disciple's ministry, but few have chosen this consecrated life.

We become a Christian when we believe and call upon the Lord Jesus to be saved. Yet the majority of Christians are content with Jesus as just their Savior but not their Lord. They are saved but not fully submitted to the Lordship of Jesus Christ.

In the New Testament, Jesus is called "Savior" less than 25 times while the name of "Lord" is found hundreds of times. Most believers do not progress to becoming a committed disciple. They are satisfied with their fire insurance policy against an eternity in hell. In the meanwhile, they live for themselves. They choose to follow after their own will and coast through a life of mediocrity.

A disciple will strive to live a separated life dedicated to pleasing God. When Martha was distracted with much serving, she was concerned about Mary who sat at Jesus' feet to hear His word. The Lord told her that Mary had "chosen that good part, which will not be taken away from her" (Luke 10:39-42). His disciples choose the "good part" when they seek His presence on the mountaintops of prayer. They enter their prayer closets to sit at the Master's feet as they seek to learn from Him, abide in His Word, and reflect His image in their actions of expression to others.

Disciples are known for their trait as ever-teachable learners. Jesus said, "If you abide in My word, you are My disciples indeed. And you shall know the truth, and the truth shall make you free" (John 8:31-32). The King James Version says, "If you continue in My word, you are My disciples indeed." Jesus said, "Blessed are those who hear the word of God and keep it!" (Luke 11:28). A disciple is someone who continues in the teachings of Jesus. A disciple is an abiding learner with an open and pliable heart for truth.

Our Lord's teachings and many parables were difficult for some of the religious establishment and the multitudes to understand but He "explained all things" to His disciples when they were alone together (Mark 4:34). His abiding Spirit within has come to enter every believer to guide us into all things, bring us in remembrance of all things and teach us things to come (John 14:26; 16:13).

Paul admonished his spiritual son Timothy, "you must continue in the things which you have learned...." He continued, "All Scripture is given by inspiration of God, and is profitable for doctrine, for reproof, for correction, for instruction in righteousness...that the man of God may be complete, thoroughly equipped for every good work" (2 Tim. 3:14-17). As we continue to do what we have learned in His Word, we will become complete and thoroughly equipped disciples and ministers, complete in His reflection to be fit for the Master's use.

True disciples also have ears that hear with a willingness to instantly obey. When Jesus beckons, we are to be like eager attendants ever ready to do His bidding. Philip, the bread server and evangelist, left a revival in Samaria to follow an angel of the Lord's command to go to the desert (Acts 8:26-30). An Ethiopian man of great authority was there sitting in his chariot reading from the book of Isaiah. The Spirit of God told Philip to "Go near and overtake this chariot." The Bible says, "Philip ran to him." He didn't walk. He didn't doubt and delay. He didn't even take time to first pray about it. Philip "went" when the Lord said "go." As a true disciple open to the Lord's call to ministry, Philip immediately obeyed by running to do God's command.

Love for One Another

Jesus said "My disciples" will be known for their "love for one another." "A new commandment I give to you, that you love one another; as I have loved you, that you also love one another. By this all will know that you are My disciples, if you have love for one another" (John 13:34-35). Three times the Lord said to "love one another" in these two verses alone. John, the apostle of love, repeatedly wrote "to love one another." This command "to love one another" is found more than fifteen times in the New Testament.

When everything is said and done, only love will last. Love is the infrastructure of everything and anything worthwhile. Long to see the day when love pours from more believers as true disciples flowing like mighty rivers of true mercy and compassion.

As we touch the realm of the Spirit of love, all dryness goes and all criticism leaves. There can be no divisions in a walk of love. The Spirit of God brings tenderness to our hearts. This is a pure, holy, and divine love that pours forth like a flood from our hearts by the Spirit within us. God has given each of us an abundant, full measure, pressed down, shaken together, and overflowing love. His disciples endeavor to be filled to overflowing with His personality, His presence, and His glorious love.

The Lord proclaimed, "I in them, and You in Me; that they may be made perfect in one, and that the world may know that You have sent Me, and have loved them as You have loved Me" (John 17:23). It is difficult to wrap our minds around the revelation fact that God loves us as much as He loves Jesus. His love is unconditional, based on who He is not on who we are. There is nothing we can do to make God love us more as there is also nothing we can do to make God love us less. Because of His character, He made the choice to love us while we were still unlovely.

His love is unchanging even if we inadequately respond to that love. God loves us the same even if we make no attempt to return that love. The quality of God's unconditional love is determined by the character of the one who loves, not the one who is being loved.

Paul expresses this perfect love,

Love suffers long and is kind; love does not envy; love does not parade itself, is not puffed up; does not behave rudely, does not seek its own, is not provoked, thinks no evil; does not rejoice in iniquity, but rejoices in the truth; bears all things, believes all things, hopes all things, endures all things. Love never fails (1 Cor. 13:4-8).

This kind of love is not a physical feeling. This pure love is not an emotional state or some abstract concept that is difficult to define. It is a choice made by the will of a believer. Love is a principle practiced as a way of life for a true disciple. This love is gentle, polite, kind, and discreet. It is self-controlled, peaceable, considerate, and slow-tempered. The God-kind of love views others as precious and valuable. This Christ-like love looks beyond an individual's present condition to see their full potential.

The love of His Spirit will trump the times the flesh wants to pay attention to evil and suffered wrongs. "Love...is not touchy or fretful or resentful; it takes no account of the evil done to it pays no attention to a suffered wrong" (1 Cor. 13:5 Amp). The old man of our previous nature will want to be like an accountant and retain the emotional baggage of touchiness and resentment. A committed disciple will put off his or her carnal nature and make the choice to side with the inner power of love by putting on the new man empowered by God's Spirit (Eph. 4:22-24).

His true love is a taste of heaven. As our mind is renewed by the Spirit of truth, we will cease to view relationships as an opportunity to get from others but rather to give. The God-kind of love will never manipulate or try to control others out of insecurity. Giving provides the greatest fulfillment that we will ever know. His love never seeks to be first or to be in control but rather assumes the place of service. Disciples are true ministers who are plugged into serving in their local assembly to reflect His compassionate love toward the brethren in obedience to be like Christ.

We can imitate God and walk in the same unconditional love. "Therefore be imitators of God as dear children. And walk in love, as Christ also has loved us and given Himself for us, an offering and a sacrifice to God for a sweet-smelling aroma" (Eph. 5:1-2). As Christ also has loved us, we can make the decision to love one another even when they unjustly hurt us.

His command is to "love your neighbor as yourself" (Gal. 5:14). At the last supper, a new command was made for us to love another as the Lord loved us. All will know and recognize His disciples by their love for one another. A true disciple's love for others will also overflow outside the walls of the church. The world will then sit up and take notice that God and His church do indeed have something to offer that they need.

Jesus revealed the Father God's love when He too was "moved with compassion" upon seeing the multitudes as weary and scattered sheep having no shepherd (Matt. 9:36-38). He saw the multitudes and the need for harvesting. The Lord then commissioned

His disciples to go and sent them out to minister (Matt. 10:1,5). His disciples will sense that same compassion and respond to His command to "go into all the world and preach the gospel to every creature" (Mark 16:15).

Disciples lay down their lives for His Great Commission to preach His glorious Gospel for salvation to a lost and unreached world. Motivated by His love and compassion, they see the multitudes through His eyes and faithfully respond to His words, "Do you not say, 'There are still four months and then comes the harvest'? Behold, I say to you, lift up your eyes and look at the fields, for they are already white for harvest!" (John 4:35).

Giving is true living. Real living is giving His love. Every outreaching local church should be a reflection of His perfect love. May the harvesting churches always be moved with His compassion and remain givers of His character and loving nature.

Reminiscent of my young son admiring a roll of duct tape for the first time, every Christian minister ought to look at the opportunity to reveal His love and say, "I like it!" We can be one of God's "worker guys," who as faithful disciples boldly proclaim and demonstrate His love. Our love motivation in expressing our ministry then is to serve and give forth to be a blessing to others. Follow Him and our instruction Book to make it our life mission to be known as one of His disciples who live to give the Gospel to the lost and His love to one another in the church.

CHAPTER 13

Release What We Have

At the conclusion of a Sunday morning service, my pastor asked everyone to find someone to pray with one-on-one. My eyes spotted a man who was a newly saved member of our church. I could tell that he wasn't comfortable with praying with anybody and was heading for the sanctuary door to make a hasty exit. I quickly intercepted him and asked what he wanted prayer for. After my prayer, I was surprised when he asked if I had a prayer request. I was in such a giving mode to pray for him that I was momentarily taken back as to what I desired prayer for. After pondering for a few seconds, I finally came up with a request for God to give me "more love" for other people.

A week later, the same man responded to an altar call. As he was prayed for, he was overwhelmed by the Spirit of God and laid on the floor for a few moments. I was coordinating the ushers that morning and was standing to one side towards the front of the sanctuary. He then got up and came straight over to me. I could tell by his eyes that he was what I would call "lost in the spirit." He pointed his finger at me and said sternly, "You have My love in you, just release it." Then he leaned his back against the wall and slid down to the floor. A few minutes later, he came to, looked up at me, and seemed befuddled as got up to hurriedly leave.

He confided with us the next Sunday, "I went to the altar for prayer and the next thing I know, I was sitting on the floor along the wall next to Fred. I couldn't remember what happened in between." While he was checked out in the Spirit, God used this babe in Christ as a yielded vessel to convey an important truth to me. I was asking for more love when God was telling me to release the love I already had. I began to search the scriptures to verify if this spiritual experience lined up with the witness of God's written Word.

John wrote that "God is love" (1 John 4:8). When we received God, we received love. When a believer asks Jesus to come into their heart, they are asking divine love to come into their spirit as well. When we received His Spirit and were born again, we also received His nature of love.

When the Lord came to dwell in our heart by His Spirit, we were made a new love creation in Christ (2 Cor. 5:17). We become temples of God's Spirit and His love (1 Cor. 3:16). His love already dwells within our spirit by the presence of the Holy Spirit. God's love was received when we received His Spirit.

"The love of God has been poured out in our hearts by the Holy Spirit who was given to us" (Rom. 5:5). Note the past tense of this verse, "the love of God HAS been poured out." Another translation renders this verse "since God's love floods our hearts through the Holy Spirit which has been given to us." His love has already been poured out in the overflow measure of a flood when we received the Holy Spirit. There is no need to ask for more as His love already floods our hearts.

Every expression of His unconditional love is already present within our hearts. He breathed His love into us when we received His Spirit. Perfect love intends to grip our entire being until it directs all our intentions, desires, and thoughts. His love was poured into us to be poured out to one another.

Jesus proclaimed that out of the hearts of believers would "flow rivers of living water" by God's Spirit (John 7:37-39). There is ever present the potential for rivers of love to pour out and flood from our hearts by the Spirit of love within every born again believer. In faith, we simply stir up and release what we already have by activating His love ever resident within us.

One question about waiting for God to answer a petition for more love is: when will the petitioner know when the "more" has arrived? Having received the Holy Spirit, a believer's heart is already flooded with His loving kindness. A Christian doesn't need more. They just need to release the love of His Spirit and become His expression the unconditional love already resident within them.

Peter and John went up together to the temple to pray when they encountered a man who had been lame from birth. Upon noticing this man in his crippled condition and expecting alms, they fixed their eyes on him. Peter said, "Look at us. Silver and gold I do not have, but what I do have I give you: In the name of Jesus Christ of Nazareth, rise up and walk." Peter took him by the right hand and lifted him up and immediately his feet and ankle bones received strength (Acts 3:1-9).

This lame man was miraculously healed by what Peter and John already had. Peter said, "What I do have I give you." They both knew what they had in the authority of the name of Love. They didn't stop and pray for more or wonder if what they had enough. There was no need to ask for more as they knew what they already had. Peter knew this and was correct to say, "What I do have I give you." Peter and John simply gave the lame man what they already had—their faith in the Lord's love and the authority of the name of Jesus Christ.

Corporate Unity

The early church experienced the expression of His love which resulted in corporate unity. Peter and John went to "their own companions" immediately after being threatened by the Pharisees when the lame man was healed (Acts 4:23). Different translations render "their own companions" as their own company, their own group, and their own friends. There is something special concerning having our own company in a local church to turn to in a time of need or crisis. We can glean something special about the unity that the early church enjoyed.

Make note of the following seven references to the unity and one accord found repeatedly with the first five chapters in the book of Acts. As they gathered in the upper room, "These all continued with one accord in prayer and supplication" (Acts 1:14). Ten days after our Lord's ascension, the promised power came as they were all still together with one accord, "When the Day of Pentecost had fully come, they were all with one accord in one place. And suddenly there came a sound from heaven, as of a rushing mighty wind, and it filled the whole house where they were sitting" (Acts 2:1-2).

Their unity in His love was again repeated in the historical account of the early church, "And all who believed—that is, who adhered to and trusted in and relied on Jesus Christ—were united, and together" (Acts 2:44 Amp). They continually met daily with one accord, "So continuing daily with one accord in the temple, and breaking bread from house to house, they ate their food with gladness and simplicity of heart" (Acts 2:46).

Their corporate praying was also with oneness, "So when they heard that, they raised their voice to God with one accord" (Acts 4:24). "Now the multitude of those who believed were of one heart and one soul" (Acts 4:32). "With one accord" is then mentioned a fifth time, "And through the hands of the apostles many signs and wonders were done among the people. And they were all with one accord in Solomon's Porch" (Acts 5:12).

These inspired biblical accounts provide us with a historical perspective that documents the successes of the early church. This account serves as an example of the importance of love and unity within a church body. In one accord within their own company, they enjoyed great power, great grace, and no lack (Acts 4:33-34). There are indeed great blessings with oneness in love to one another as we unite in one body and one Spirit.

John, the apostle of love, gave two commands to "believe on the name of His Son Jesus Christ and love one another" (1 John

3:23). God's unity requirements are simple, believe in Jesus, and believe in love. Even if we might disagree on some theological doctrine, we can do so without becoming disagreeable. We can agree to disagree while continuing to believe in our expression of oneness with Jesus and one another. Oneness will not fuss over issues that are not important. The unity love brings will find a point of agreement in Christ and build from that foundation.

Forgiveness

We are to be kind to one another and forgive as God forgave us. "And become useful and helpful and kind to one another, tenderhearted (compassionate, understanding, loving-hearted), forgiving one another (readily and freely), as God in Christ forgave you" (Eph. 4:32 Amp). What matters is that we by faith choose God's way of love, peace, kindness, and forgiveness toward one another. We are to be ever quick to freely forgive one another supernaturally by expressing His indwelling Spirit of love.

One key aspect of the process of any emotional recovery and reconciliation involves forgiving, praying for the offender, and thereby letting the offense go. Our thoughts and intent for that person will change as we reflect His love and pray like our Lord's example, "Forgive them, for they know not what they do" (Luke 23:34, Acts 7:60). When pride and ego side with our hurt and suffering, our feelings and emotions will never heal. Let's allow the Holy Spirit to shut the door to resentment, offense, bitterness, and strife. We need to stay sensitive to the Holy One by not allowing unresolved conflicts, hostilities, past grudges, ill-will, animosities, or anger to build up and defile our hearts. We can choose to live in bondage to bitterness or enjoy the freedom of loving forgiveness. We have the choice of our will to either continue to allow the bitterness to reign over us, or we can get over it and move on as a reflection of His loving expressions.

In One Accord

The night before His suffering and death on the cross, Jesus was praying for His disciples and for us to know the same intimacy of oneness that He has eternally known with God the Father.

I do not pray for these alone, but also for those who will believe in Me through their word; that they all may be one, as You, Father, are in Me, and I in You; that they also may be one in Us, that the world may believe that You sent Me. And the glory which You gave Me I have given them, that they may be one just as We are one: I in them, and You in Me; that they may be made perfect in one, and that the world may know that You have sent Me, and have loved them as You have loved Me (John 17:20-23).

His prayer was answered when we received "the harmony and oneness of [produced by] the Spirit in the binding power of peace" into one body, Spirit, hope, Lord, faith, baptism, and Father God of us all (Eph. 4:3-6 Amp). This portion of scripture mentions "one" on seven occasions—one body, one Spirit, one hope, one Lord, one faith, one baptism, and one God. Seven is God's number for perfection. By His Spirit, the church is baptized into one body, the body of Christ. In Christ, we become one with God and with one another as part of His one Spirit of love.

As one body, we are to stand fast in one Spirit as we strive together in Him for the faith of the Gospel. With a mutual identity of purpose, we are to be like-minded, living in harmony, and having the same love. As our hearts beat in unison, we will have the same mind, purpose and attitude of Christ. We can walk in one accord with God and other believers, knowing that He made us all as one, as the Father and the Son are one. His one love will work in us perfectly and bind us together in unity. His power is energized, operated, and governed by His unconditional love within us.

We are commanded to love one another as He first loved us.

We are all called as His ministers of expression to bring His love, grace, and glory into this earth as emptied-of-self vessels overflowing with His joy, peace, and life. His pure love pours through us with tenderhearted mercy that touches the heart of mankind with the desire of God. Our hands become implements of His kindness. Our lips rain forth with His compassion. Our attitudes are rich demonstrations of forgiveness and mercy. Our actions speak forth volumes by His perfect, unconditional love.

This motivating force of oneness creates within us an intense love for God and other Christians. His love wells up within and overflows as rivers of living water toward those around us. We are driven to be conduits, overflowing with His compassion to discover the expressive ministry of every Christian in serving and freely giving to others. We are God's faithful stones laid upon His foundation where Christ is the Cornerstone building, a church framed by unity. With one heart and soul, the church reflects His life in its highest form by pouring forth His abundant love. In the expression of His love, we glorify the Lord in one love, with one mind, in one accord toward one another.

Paul encouraged Timothy to stir up the gift of the Holy Spirit that He already had in him. "Therefore I remind you to stir up the gift of God which is in you through the laying on of my hands. For God has not given us a spirit of fear, but of power and of love and of a sound mind" (2 Tim. 1:6-7). The gift Timothy received was God's Spirit of love. God expects His church to stir up and release the love already living within. This verse is also past tense. The Spirit of love "has" been given to every born again believer.

Since He has done it, there is no need for a believer to pray for something already in their possession. Having already received His Spirit of love, there's no need to ask for more. When we possess His Spirit, we already have all His love within. We need to allow His Spirit of love to possess us. When He floods our heart, His love floods our heart. The complete and perfect package of love arrived when we received the gift of His Spirit.

102

It's not scriptural for a believer to pray for more love. Months, years, and decades from now, they will still be praying that same prayer with no answer from heaven. How can God give someone more when he or she already has all they need? Even if God gave them more, how will they know if that's enough? When a believer is already filled with His Spirit, where will the "more" go? How can we pour more into an already full vessel? There are popular worship songs that ask the Holy Spirit to fall and dwell in us. We sing and pray for God to give more of Himself to us. This must seem strange to a God who has previously answered those requests since His Spirit of love came to abide in us when we were first saved. Imagine what a parent might think for a child who keeps asking for a gift that is already in their possession.

His Spirit of love already abides in us. Look within for what's already there. This love is not a goose bump physical feeling or an emotional state but a force latent in our spirits with ever-present potential to be activated and released.

Don't wait for a rebuke out of the mouth of a babe in Christ saying, "You have My love in you, just release it!" We already have His Spirit and His love. His love floods our heart by the Holy Spirit. We begin our love ministry of expression when we give the Gift of the Holy Spirit whom we have already received. Now is the time to stir up what we already have and release the power of His love toward one another.

CHAPTER 14

To Not or Not To Not

Our entire family enjoys watching football on television. When Kyle was just a baby, he took notice of the football game that was on the screen. For the next thirty minutes, he said, "Ouch!" every time a player was tackled.

Later when our boys were eight- and five-years-old, we were all making note of the physicality in the game of football. We asked Kyle if he wanted to play football some day. He quickly replied, "No, I don't want to be tackled." We asked the younger Myles if he was going to play tackle football. His response was, "Yeah, 'cause they're NOT going to able to catch me to tackle me!"

We can learn from the "not" instructions in the Bible. We have a choice whether to "not" or not to "not."

Companies employ troubleshooters to locate problems and make repairs in machinery or technical equipment. They go through a systemic process to locate the trouble by eliminating what it's not. One way to learn how to do something correctly is to observe examples of how not to do it.

I have learned how to become a better athlete, coach, teacher, manager, administrator, and pastor by my observations from good mentors. I have also learned as much about how not to do some things by observing and learning from sub-par mentors. We learn how to appropriately act toward one another by how God's Word tells us not to act. Here are some of the one another verses on how we are "not" to treat other believers in the Lord.

Do not grumble against one another, brethren, lest you be condemned. Behold, the Judge is standing at the door! (Jam. 5:9).

Do not lie to one another (Col. 3:9).

Not returning evil for evil or reviling for reviling, but on the contrary blessing, knowing that you were called to this, that you may inherit a blessing (1 Pet. 3:9).

Do not use liberty as an opportunity for the flesh, but through love serve one another (Gal. 5:13).

It is already an utter failure for you that you go to law against one another (1 Cor. 6:7).

But if you bite and devour another, beware lest you be consumed by one another! (Gal. 5:15).

Let us not become conceited, provoking one another, envying one another (Gal. 5:26).

These last two verses are like a couple of bookend scriptures as the introductory and conclusion statements that Paul writes to the Galatians about walking in the Spirit and the fruit of the spirit. Right after Paul informs us about consuming one another if we bite and devour another in verse 15, he proceeds in the next verse to exhort us to walk in the spirit. He again tells us later in verse 25 to walk in the spirit followed immediately by verse 26 to "not become conceited, provoking one another, envying one another." Our attitudes and actions toward one another will determine any success in truly walking in the Spirit.

We are to "shun profane and idle babblings, for they will increase to more ungodliness. And their message will spread like cancer" (2 Tim. 2:16-17). Cancer of the human body is character-ized by uncontrolled, disorderly cell growth. It is called a tumor when a mass of these cells develops. The tumor may become malignant and spread from the original site to another location in a process called metastasis. The ability of cancerous cells to metasta-size makes early detection critical.

To "bite and devour another" has the similar effect to the body of Christ as does uncontrolled, disorderly cell growth to the human body. They both have similar results as the body is consumed by the uncontrolled behavior. Like a cancer, our ill-will metastasizes to other members of the body of Christ by our disorderly grumbling, lying, giving evil for evil and reviling for reviling, provoking, envying, biting, and devouring of one another. There should be

> *no schism in the body, but that the members should have the same care for one another. And if one member suffers, all the members suffer with it; or if one member is honored, all the members rejoice with it. Now you are the body of Christ, and members individually* (1 Cor. 12:25-27).

The definition of schism is a formal division in or separation from a church or religious body.

We are all members of the same body who are to "care for one another." It would be extremely disruptive if any schism of the members of our physical body did not work together. For example, the fingers on our hand work together for the common good of the hand and the rest of the body.

Divine Order

The reflection of His love toward one another becomes the essence of divine order that brings the church together where there is no schism in His body but a perfect blending of heart to heart. The expressions of His perfect love manifest the sweetness of our association with Christ.

The Apostle Paul's heart was for a love spirit of unity to be expressed within the church. He wrote, "May the God who gives endurance and encouragement give you a spirit of unity among yourselves as you follow Christ Jesus" (Rom. 15:5 NIV). Our love interaction with one another within our own church is what determines whether we are truly in one accord. We are to strive toward unity within the community of our local church. Like the early church, we too are built powerfully by unity and love.

The fruit of this unification of one was evident as in a mathematic equation of addition then multiplication. The converts were first added to the church, "Then those who gladly received his word were baptized; and that day about three thousand souls were added to them" (Acts 2:41). Then they were added daily, "And the Lord added to the church daily those who were being saved" (Acts 2:47). Later, believers were added, "And believers were increasingly added to the Lord, multitudes of both men and women" (Acts 5:14). Then the increase switched from souls being added to their being multiplied, "Then the word of God spread, and the number of the disciples multiplied greatly in Jerusalem, and a great many of the priests were obedient to the faith" (Acts 6:7).

In the expression of unity and love found in the early church, the progression of souls went from "added" to "added to the church daily" to "increasingly added" to "multiplied greatly." That's exponential growth of salvations in this environment of loving one another among believers. There's power in unity. The devil knows that. That's why he attempts to continually planting seeds of strife and division within any fruitful ministry. He takes the differences between us, even the differences put there by God to make us stronger, and uses them as a wedge to drive us apart.

It is the cohesiveness of groups of Christians with shared interests and lifestyles that build unity. As we locate our own company, local church unity springs from partnership, intimacy, responsibility, and relationships together with one another. It is a mistake to profess to be partners with God but not with other Christian saints who also have the same God in them. The people are the purpose for our ministry.

Paul prayed for believers, "That you may with one mind and one mouth glorify the God and Father of our Lord Jesus Christ" (Rom. 15:6). We need to be like-minded, having the same love toward one another by being one in spirit and purpose and doing nothing out of selfish ambition or vain conceit. In humility, we should look not only to our own interests but also to the interests of others. His will is for us to be in one accord through corporate unity. We are to "stand fast in one spirit" as the body of the living God unified by His love (Phil. 1:27). Paul continued, "Fulfill my joy by being like-minded, having the same love, being of one accord, of one mind" (Phil. 2:2).

We need to have the same humble attitude as Christ. Let's follow Christ's example by walking and flowing in love. As we touch the realm of the love of His Spirit, any critical heart will want to leave. There are no divisions with life in His Spirit. As we enter the realm of unity with Him, all criticism of one another leaves. We are to flow as one with one another. We avoid division, strife, and confusion by choosing the power of oneness, love, and unity. As we choose by faith to walk in the Spirit of love, we close the door to disunity. Division is the result when we lack His vision of love for another.

Recognizing Authority

It is easy to spot those with contempt for leadership within the church "especially those who walk according to the flesh in the lust of uncleanness and despise authority. They are presumptuous, self-willed. They are not afraid to speak evil of dignitaries" (2 Pet. 2:10). They openly "despise authority" by speaking perverse things in a condescending fashion toward pastors and church leaders. They are "not afraid to speak evil of dignitaries" or to those in authority within the church. Their presumptuous attitudes are obvious in their brazen, outspoken, and candid remarks that belittle authority figures. They are self-willed, which shows an arrogant determination to go their own way and do whatever they want, at any cost, to themselves or to anyone else. They love to attack, defame, disdain, and humiliate those who are in authority, usually in accusing them of a lack of spirituality.

Don't confuse their arrogance with boldness. In their brazenness, they are walking "according to the flesh in the lust of uncleanness." Recognize it for what it is—cancer-like remarks that are rude, harsh, and sarcastic. Such accusations will cause one to fall in line with a trait of the devil. Satan is also known as the "accuser of our brethren" (Rev. 12:10). Such perverse speech is according to the flesh and not the fruit of the Spirit of love.

Keep clear of those who openly and quickly criticize to tear down pastoral leadership. To even take part by listening to such perversity puts us in a position of gossiping about or even slandering their church leader. Like a cancer, gossip is a destructive force that God will not abide in. The end result of any action taken should always be that the individual and the church are edified.

I personally enjoy learning from both church and secular history. Occasionally, I will watch the History Channel on television. I was horrified with watching a particular television documentary on war crimes in the Pacific during World War II. Mostly driven by hunger, infantry troops cannibalized the dead bodies of enemy soldiers. They were consuming their livers and cutting off arms and legs for future meals. Because of this, there were many violent reprisal acts to enemy prisoners in retaliation.

As a culture, we find human cannibalism to be appalling, yet isn't it the same when we bite and devour one another in the body of Christ? We are in effect consuming one another when we respond negatively by our carnal flesh. We are to put off the old man with his deeds and put on the new man created within by God's Spirit (Eph. 4:22-24). As we are sensitive to our recreated spirit and His indwelling Spirit of love, we will have a check in our heart against consuming one another in the church with our words or our actions.

Whenever we take communion, we need to have discernment in our judgments concerning the Lord's body. Paul wrote,

For I received from the Lord that which I also delivered to you: that the Lord Jesus on the same night in which He was betrayed

took bread; and when He had given thanks, He broke it and said, "Take, eat; this is My body which is broken for you; do this in remembrance of Me." In the same manner He also took the cup after supper, saying, "This cup is the new covenant in My blood. This do, as often as you drink it, in remembrance of Me." For as often as you eat this bread and drink this cup, you proclaim the Lord's death till He comes. Therefore whoever eats this bread or drinks this cup of the Lord in an unworthy manner will be guilty of the body and blood of the Lord. But let a man examine himself, and so let him eat of the bread and drink of the cup. For he who eats and drinks in an unworthy manner eats and drinks judgment to himself, not discerning the Lord's body. For this reason many are weak and sick among you, and many sleep. For if we would judge ourselves, we would not be judged. But when we are judged, we are chastened by the Lord, that we may not be condemned with the world (1 Cor. 11:23-32).

Communion is sacred when we remember His physical body that suffered greatly in our place with His scourging and His death on the cross. We also need to judge ourselves in our discernment of how we relate to His spiritual body, the church. We drink judgment on ourselves when we fail to discern our evil judgments and actions toward the body of Christ.

As we judge ourselves in the Lord, we will not be judged. We are to examine ourselves before the Lord to seek His judgment where we may have failed to honor and love the members of His church. Let's take communion in a worthy manner and not eat or drink judgment upon ourselves.

We need to repent and seek the chastening by the Lord as He will deal with us spiritually as sons where we may have transgressed toward one another. Let's go to church services not to devour or be consumed, but rather to comfort one another, encourage one another, edify one another, strengthen one another, and build each other up. We have the capacity to comfort one another by the enablement of the Comforter within us, the Holy Spirit.

Many can quote Luke 6:38 as a promise of financial returns for our giving without considering the proceeding verses. But the context has nothing to do with the subject of money. Jesus said,

> *But I say to you who hear...love your enemies, do good, and lend, hoping for nothing in return; and your reward will be great, and you will be sons of the Most High. For He is kind to the unthankful and evil. Therefore be merciful, just as your Father also is merciful. Judge not, and you shall not be judged. Condemn not, and you shall not be condemned. Forgive, and you will be forgiven. Give, and it will be given to you: good measure, pressed down, shaken together, and running over will be put into your bosom. For with the same measure that you use, it will be measured back to you* (Luke 6:27,35-38).

We can give love, kindness, mercy and forgiveness, or judgment, condemnation, and unforgiveness toward others. The Bible promises that we will reap what we have sown (Galatians 6:7-8). We can either sow bad weed seeds or good love seeds. Our harvest will be what we have planted. What we give will be given back to us.

As His dear children, let us imitate our heavenly Father and speak in love to the rest of His children in our family. Out of our mouths as His babes, we'll speak and demonstrate His love in our ministry to the church. Then we will NOT be consuming one another within the body of Christ. The devil will not be given the opportunity to catch us in his snares as we carry the ball of love for touchdowns with one another in the Lord. We will give love and mercy; it will be given back to us in good measure, pressed down, shaken together, and running over.

CHAPTER 15

Arrogant Anarchists

A young boy kept standing on his family's new couch with his shoes on. His exasperated father told him for the third time to sit down. The boy reluctantly relented and sit with crossed arms and pouting lips. He then exclaimed in a defiant tone, "I may be sitting down on the outside, but I'm still standing up on the inside!"

How often there are similar responses by immature Christians within the Father God's church toward authority figures! With a non-Christlike reflection of attitude, some believers defiantly protest submission to authority. Their heart is not right in their inward defiance to designated church leadership.

We are all instructed to "submitting to one another in the fear of the Lord" (Eph. 5:21). True submission causes us to be humbly compliant to the authority of another while mock submission is done out of prideful arrogance of those who won't submit to the authority that the Lord has given within His church.

From the biblical perspective of submission and authority, there are a those in the body of Christ whom I have called arrogant anarchists. An anarchist is one who rebels against any authority, established order, or ruling power.

Non-submission tendencies are associated with pride in the Bible, "Likewise you younger people, submit yourselves to your elders. Yes, all of you be submissive to one another, and be clothed with humility, for 'God resists the proud, but gives grace to the humble'" (1 Pet. 5:5). There are believers who choose to "be clothed with humility" and those who are arrogantly proud. We have the choice to either reflect humility or pride. God resists the

112

proud and gives grace to the humble who are submitted. The trademark of true humility is when we are "submissive to one another."

Obedience

A typically arrogant anarchist will claim to only submit to God but not to man. Yet in their non-submission to church leadership, they are not truly submitted to God's Word. They boast about how only God is "over" them. Such claims not only reveal their arrogance but also their ignorance of scriptural principles established repeatedly in the New Testament. The Bible frequently refers to "overseers" and those who are "over" us in positions of authority and leadership.

We are told to "obey those who rule over you, and be submissive, for they watch out for your souls, as those who must give account. Let them do so with joy and not with grief, for that would be unprofitable for you" (Heb. 13:17). It is obvious from this scripture that God expects obedience to those who He has placed "over" us to "watch out" for our souls. We're to obey our leaders and defer to them in the Lord.

The New International Version renders that verse, "Obey your leaders and submit to their authority." Notice the closing statement of this verse found in another translation, "Obey your leaders and give way to them; they watch over your souls because they must give an account of them; make this a joy for them to do, and not a grief—you yourselves would be the losers." For one not to belong to a flock in submission to the overseers who the Holy Spirit has placed over that flock, they will be, according to this verse, the losers in their disobedience.

Some view themselves as too spiritual to need a leader. That is arrogance and pride gone to seed that will proceed an inevitable fall (Prov. 16:18). Which is worse, not to obey and submit to those who God has placed over them or not to have those over them to obey and submit to? One can't obey and give way to leaders whom they do not have. Both of these scenarios are wrong and examples of rebellion, pride, and unbelief.

The Lord's Shepherds

Having served as a pastor, I was ever watchful of "Lone Ranger" Christians who were not hooked up properly to a church. Church leaders can relate to Paul's heart when he said,

> *For I have not shunned to declare to you the whole counsel of God. Therefore take heed to yourselves and to all the flock, among which the Holy Spirit has made you overseers, to shepherd the church of God which He purchased with His own blood. For I know this, that after my departure savage wolves will come in among you, not sparing the flock. Also from among yourselves men will rise up, speaking perverse things, to draw away the disciples after themselves. Therefore watch, and remember that for three years I did not cease to warn everyone night and day with tears (Acts 20:27-31).*

Paul admonished this group of overseers and elders as the host of a pastor's conference in the verses above. Make note of his statement to them, "take heed to yourselves and to all the flock, among which the Holy Spirit has made you overseers." Paul proclaimed this after saying that he had "not shunned to declare to you the whole counsel of God." Paul, in the context of declaring the whole counsel of God, charged the "overseers, to shepherd the church of God." It was the Holy Spirit Himself who made each of these leader's overseers "to all the flock" as the Lord's representatives to tend the Great Shepherd's sheep who were "purchased with His own blood." By the Holy Spirit, an overseer is placed in their position of leadership in ministry to demonstrate His love by taking the Lord's mantle of a pastor to shepherd His sheep and lambs. He sets those in leadership to watch over the well-being of His church.

The Lord asked Peter three times, "Simon, son of Jonah, do you love Me?" Peter's love would be proven as He honored His three commands to, "Feed My lambs. Tend My sheep. Feed My sheep" (John 21:15-17). In their love for Christ, Peter and all pastoral overseers are to have the Father's heart to lovingly feed and tend the sheep and lambs in their flocks. The Holy Spirit is not sending hirelings but loving under-shepherds to care for the church. Paul's compassion for God's flock was evident as he said to the overseers, "Take heed…I did not cease to warn everyone night and day with tears."

Jesus gives gifts to men for the equipping, maturing, and edification of His flocks. A careful study of the fourth chapter in Ephesians will reveal the cost of not receiving these gifts which include the grace and office of a pastor. First of all, an arrogant anarchist will not be equipped to maturity. As a non-submitted part of His body, they will not be fully edified or come to the unity of the faith. They will be as losers who won't grow up in all things into Him who is the head, Christ. Their adolescent and prideful attitude will keep them from maturing to spiritual adulthood.

Jesus gave the gift of a pastor-teacher to keep us from becoming like "children, tossed to and fro and carried about with every wind of doctrine, by the trickery of men, in the cunning craftiness of deceitful plotting" (Eph. 4:14). Some teenagers go through a stage when they think they are smarter than their parents. They know just enough to be dangerous. This is an example of spiritual adolescent arrogance to think one has all the necessary knowledge and is too spiritual to need a covering.

Submission to Jesus as the head of the body of Christ and to His appointed leadership in His body brings unity, growth, and spiritual maturity. Such maturity is a process not an arrival. It is a journey ever traveled, not a destination ever reached in this life. With more maturity comes the realization of how far we have yet to go. Our walk toward maturity is to ever strive to reflect and release His character within as the fruit of His Spirit transforms our souls (emotions and mind) into the likeness and image of Christ.

Recognize the necessity in being a part of His body. He intends for all to have under-shepherds to watch over His flock from the "savage wolves" that will "rise up, speaking perverse things, to draw away the disciples after themselves." Paul warned of the vulnerability of the flock to "savage wolves" and "perverse" men drawing them away.

We need to stay clear of so-called "deep sheep" whose special gifts or revelations are too superior to submit to any church overseer, pastor, or leader. Likewise, let's be prayerful about receiving any ministry from these "loose cannon" ministers (i.e. parking lot prophesiers) who are not accountable to obey other legitimate spiritual coverings. What right does an individual have to speak into other people's lives when they're not willing to likewise allow an overseer to speak into their own? Why submit to the authority of one who is not likewise submitted to the authority of another.

Such are often puffed up by pride from either their special gifts or from the depths of their spiritual knowledge to find a church worthy of their self-disillusionary stature. It is nothing more than arrogant anarchy to fall into the deception of thinking that one is too spiritual to need a pastor.

The Lord taught,

> *He who receives you receives Me, and he who receives Me receives Him who sent Me. He who receives a prophet in the name of a prophet shall receive a prophet's reward. And he who receives a righteous man in the name of a righteous man shall receive a righteous man's reward* (Matt. 10:40-41).

When we receive the person the Lord sends, then we are receiving the Lord. When we are rejecting His gift, then we are rejecting the Giver of that gift. There is a reward to be received when we receive the gift of an overseer that the Holy Spirit sends into our life. God gives the gift of an under-shepherd with His heart to feed, tend, and care for our well-being.

Where there is no covering and no accountability, there's a great possibility for lawlessness and a rebellious heart. Be watchful for those perverse persons who seek to draw others away from God's appointed authority.

Critical Spirits

It is too easy to sit back like armchair quarterbacks from their seats and second guess a church service or a sermon presentation. The arrogant anarchist spews their unkind, sharp-tongued observations about what they would have done if they were the one in charge. They appoint themselves as judge, prosecutor, and jury to pronounce their sentences of condemnation.

The result is that pastors are getting verbally abused by people with immature character flaws. Even though most of these people have never conducted one service, their arrogance as spiritual "experts" compels them to believe that they know more about ministry and the realm of the Spirit.

Such negative critiques not only poison and defile their soul with bitterness, but they will then make it their self-appointed crusade to plant their seeds of discord and strife in any ear that will listen. As agents of division within the body of Christ, they make victims of others who are influenced by their accusations. The small seeds of arrogance, pride and rebellion will produce a harvest of an anarchist with unhealthy independence and resistance to authority.

There are "savage wolves" who desire to be seen by men and be in control. They attend a new church looking for access to the microphone in the pulpit or perhaps from within the music ministry. They have no interest in serving in the more menial assignments that are not seen by men. They are looking for a platform to share their revelations.

When these ambitions aren't met to their satisfaction, they are then "led" to go to another church. As they depart, they usually plant seeds of discord by firing parting verbal salvos against their previous pastor's leadership abilities. Their bitterness is soothed as they burn yet another bridge behind them.

They eventually become so embittered that there is no pastor worthy of their mock submission. They may live in an area that has tens maybe even hundreds of churches and pastors listed in the phone book, but they feel that there is no flesh and blood person worthy of their spirituality. They develop an unhealthy view of church leadership. They then seek to rescue others from pastors and spiritual accountability.

Watch those who refuse to submit, to change, to heed counsel, and to believe that they were wrong in any of their actions or words. It is spiritual pride when one is not accountable to a covering. If any person cannot submit to authority—specifically to a local church and a local pastor—then they should not be ministering to His flock. We are not to be independent ministers but ministers who are interdependent upon one another.

All ministers need fellow ministers. Even Paul, as the author of much of the New Testament, went to those of reputation to judge his ministry (Gal. 2:1-10). Paul admonished that prophecies be judged by the other ministers who were present (1 Cor. 14:29). A secure minister will welcome the scrutiny from other ministers of reputation.

We are all to:

> *remember those who rule over you, who have spoken the word of God to you, whose faith follow, considering the outcome of their conduct. Jesus Christ is the same yesterday, today, and forever. Do not be carried about with various and strange doctrines* (Heb. 13:7-9).

As we "remember those who rule over" us, their lifestyle will motivate us to the reward in serving a God who never changes. They are those "whose faith" we are to "follow."

The arrogantly immature, who lack a full grasp of this aspect of the whole counsel of God, will counter with "I follow no man, only Christ." Paul talked of how he made himself to the church as "an example of how you should follow us" (2 Thess. 3:9). Paul told the church at Corinth to, "Imitate me, just as I also imitate Christ" (1 Cor. 11:1). We are to "imitate those who through faith and patience inherit the promises" (Heb. 6:12).

It is alright to follow those who follow Jesus by the expression of their example and lifestyles. We are following Christ as we follow and imitate the ministry gifts whom He gives us. God places leaders over us as examples for imitation of Christ. They are gifts who minister God's Word so we are not being "carried about with various and strange doctrines."

Some Lead Others Astray

Be leery of self-appointed Bible studies or independent cell groups that are led by persons with no covering, umbrella, or sounding board of reputable and established ministers. Without a covering, they become like little trees with no shade or protection from every wind of doctrine. Such exposed individuals will sooner or later go off on spiritual tangents of error, excess, or effort.

It is easy to spot such types with their new and deep revelations that draw more attention to themselves than to the Lord. Too often we hear the "God told me" statements with their "various and strange doctrines" that can't be backed up with scripture. From their little isolated caves, they fall into an Elijah syndrome with disillusionments of self-importance proclaiming, "I alone am left" (1 Kings 19:10,14). God told Elijah the contrary as He had "reserved" seven thousand others in Israel that had not bowed their knees to Baal (1 Kings 19:18). Elijah was not the only one left.

"For you were like sheep going astray, but have now returned to the Shepherd and Overseer of your souls" (1 Pet. 2:25). My prayer is that anarchist believers who are astray in their arrogant caves will have Elijah-like discernment to hear God's voice saying to them, "What are you doing here?" They are not the only one as God has reserved thousands of overseers for all of His flock who can faithfully feed and care for them.

As we find our flock, return to our fold, and submit to the overseer that the Great Shepherd and Overseer has placed over us, we watch out for our soul and we are on our way to becoming a balanced and maturing believer. Unlike the young boy who wanted to stand on the family furniture, we can obey our Father God's instructions on how to humbly submit and minister to those He has placed over us and conduct ourselves properly in the household of faith.

CHAPTER 16

Just Right Tators

Most churches have members like the Tator family where each individual differs in their own unique identity and distinct personality.

Richard, the husband and father of the Tator family, is better known to all at church as Dick. Dick Tator insists on being the self-appointed boss. He always tells everyone what to do. Dick wants to be chairman of the deacons and in charge of the personnel committee. When he can't dictate, Dick won't even come to church at all. His personality is just like his younger brother, Poten Tator, as they both desire to be the big shots.

His wife, Hezzie Tator, always says she will assist at church but somehow just never gets around to actually delivering her promised help. She hesitates and often says, "I should but..." Hezzie's confident that she will someday serve the Lord and His church.

Hezzie's sister and brother-in-law rarely attend church services. Whipped Tator works all week and sleeps in on her weekends. On Sunday mornings, Couch Tator prefers to lounge on the sofa and watch his favorite sporting events.

Dick and Hezzie have four teenagers known as the "Tator Chips" and two young children that the workers in the church nursery affectionately call the "Tator Tots."

Their oldest daughter, Emma Tator, is the member of the family who follows all the latest fads. She is more worried about what she wears to church than she is about what happens there. Emma has yet to discover her own identity in Christ because she's always busy trying to pretend to be like someone else.

Their other teenage daughter, Carmen Tator, has an opinion about everything as you never need to ask what she thinks because she's the first one to tell you. She offers critical commentary about the way things are done around the church. Carmen goes by the nickname Roe. Roe Tator is also ever trying to get other people to change things to her liking.

Neither of their twin sons (Speck Tator and Agie Tator) wants to get involved either. Speck's favorite phrase is, "I love work. I can watch others do it for hours." He doesn't get involved, but he's a great observer and spectator. Of course, if they don't do it to suit him, he will surely be the first to criticize and find fault. Agie Tator is in continual conflict with others and always seems to be involved in strife and division. His primary trait is that he doesn't play well with others. No matter what the pastor or church does, it's never good enough in Agie's eyes.

Speck, Agie, Emma and Carmen all sit in the back pews of the church to cause problems with their three adolescent cousins—Irri Tator, Debili Tator, and Devas Tator.

The church pastor greatly appreciates Dick's uncle and two aunts who are considered the pillars of their church. Orient Tator, Implemen Tator, and Facili Tator are always faithful to save the day and make things easier by encouraging everyone to pull together.

Everyone's favorite, though, is Sweet Po Tator. She always has something nice to say about everyone. Sweet Po Tator is the ideal member of the church known for her faithfulness and loyalty. Best of all, she doesn't ever dictate, hesitate, imitate, commentate, or agitate.

Obviously, we don't want to be imitators of the selfish members of the Tator family. Instead of being carnal Tators after the old nature, we are to "be imitators of God as dear children" (Eph. 5:1). We are to put on the new man as a reflection of the nature of God we received as a new creation in Christ,

That you put off, concerning your former conduct, the old man

which grows corrupt according to the deceitful lusts, and be renewed in the spirit of your mind, and that you put on the new man which was created according to God, in true righteousness and holiness. Therefore, putting away lying, "Let each one of you speak truth with his neighbor," for we are members of one another (Eph. 4:22-25).

Balanced, Biblical Submission

Thank God that there are believers with the right balance to biblical submission and authority. They are what Goldilocks called "just right" in the popular children's nursery story. The young Goldilocks found the mother and father bear's beds and chairs to be "too hard" and "too soft." She declared their porridges to be "too hot" and "too cold." But the baby bear's porridge, chair, and bed were all "just right." Our goal is to find this just right balance with our submission toward God's authority within the church.

As a pastor, I so appreciated the saints in our congregation who are just right as both submitted and committed in their expressions to God and to one another. Balanced believers on their way to just right maturity are submitted to "walk worthy...with all lowliness and gentleness, with longsuffering, bearing with one another in love." They have committed themselves in "endeavoring to keep the unity of the Spirit in the bond of peace" (Eph. 4:1-3).

In their committed submission to God, they honor Him by their actions and attitudes in their ministry to the leaders God has placed over them. They are not too formal or too casual in their interaction with church leadership. There is an ease when they are in each other's presence. They are fully submitted to God, which is demonstrated by a walk toward one another marked by lowliness, gentleness, and longsuffering. They endeavor to keep the unity and peace by their quality decision to bear with one another in love.

"Submitting to one another in the fear of the Lord" (Eph. 5:21). Our submission to one another is motivated by our reverential awe of God grace. "But He gives more grace. Therefore He says: 'God resists the proud, but gives grace to the humble.' Therefore submit to God. Resist the devil and he will flee from you" (Jam. 4:6-7). The balanced believer receives the "grace" and "more grace" that God gives because of their humility to submit.

Many will quote only the second half of verse 7, "Resist the devil and he will flee from you." We can't omit the first part of that verse which is the prerequisite to our resisting. We must first be submitted to God before our resistance will make the devil flee. Resistance is futile if we are not first submitted to God. His grace will cause the devil to flee when we are submitted to God.

We are not submitted to God if we are not submitted to one another and to church authority. Our submission to God will be reflected in our submission to one another. True submission is shown by our humility toward all men. God resists us when we are too proud to submit to church leadership. When we are humble and submitted, God's grace is given for us to resist the devil. We can resist or be resisted by our decision to be humble or proud.

True humility is shown by our subjection and obedience to God's appointed authority.

> *Remind the people to be subject to rulers and authorities, to be obedient, to be ready to do whatever is good, to slander no one, to be peaceable and considerate, and to show true humility to all men* (Titus 3:1-2 NIV).

Just right Tator's are subject to the rulers and authorities whom God has placed in their church. They are obedient and ever ready to do whatever is good toward one another. Balanced believers are peaceable and considerate as their words and actions show true humility to all men. They will slander no one nor listen to the slander of another. It is certainly not a compliment to our character if others will anticipate that we will take their side in their judgmental statements concerning church leadership. Steer clear of those who preface such statements with, "Promise not to tell the pastor this but...."

Sweet Po Tators endeavor to keep the unity of the Spirit in the bond of peace. Their true blue traits include meekness by staying teachable. They humbly stay submitted to God and His leadership—even when they are in positions of leadership. They follow God. They also follow His delegated leadership as they follow God. They are committed to unity with the flock at their local church. They have layers of authority and accountability with friends, peers, and a pastoral team to speak into their life. They are surrounded and protected by wise counsel with their covering and close Christian friends at their sides. Their local church becomes like a tree of refuge and an oasis from the world.

"Let the elders who rule well be counted worthy of double honor, especially those who labor in the word and doctrine" (1 Tim. 5:17). They appreciate the leadership who labor well in the Word and doctrine with double honor. They are submitted to the Spirit of God and to the overseer whom He has placed in their church. They are committed to give their time and finances to support their local church. They have fully received with double honor the pastor gift who rules well in their church. The balanced recognize those who labor over them and purpose "to esteem them very highly in love for their work's sake" (1 Thess. 5:12,13).

Balanced believers understand that submission is not doing what both we and our leader want done. That's agreement not submission. Submission is doing what another wants when we don't want to do it. One's true colors are shown when one is asked to do something they don't want to.

The correct balance also includes not being a doormat to leadership with no opportunity to ask for clarification. When the angel Gabriel appeared to Mary, she asked, "How can this be, since I know not a man?" (Luke 1:34). When Ananias spoke to Jesus in a vision about Saul, he questioned, "Lord, I have heard from many about this man, how much harm he has done to Your saints in Jerusalem" (Acts 9:10-18). Gabriel or the Lord did not rebuke their legitimate inquiries.

A secure and balanced leader will listen and be open to helpful suggestions when it's appropriate. They will respond to thoughtful questions and concerns. It's good to be surrounded with respectful persons and wise counsel. They won't come back with some callous "cause I said so" type of response. There should be room for necessary inquiry. A considerate leader will listen but also expect full cooperation with their final requests.

In an effort to save money, our congregation did all the labor in the remodeling of our church sanctuary except for the electrical work and the carpet installation. With the oversight of our architect, who was also a licensed general contractor, I acted as the on-site rookie general contractor. I would listen to the many suggestions from the church members who volunteered their efforts. I valued their advice, but at times had to ask them to submit to some of my decisions that they didn't always agree with. For me, as a novice to such endeavors, it was amateur hour at best, but we survived the challenges of our construction project in their submission to my leadership decisions.

Balanced believers understand the importance of expressing their ministry to one another under the covering of a pastor. They do not want to do anything that would hurt another church member. They are not loose cannons looking for some opportunity to straighten out leadership and bring division or confusion to the flock.

As true supportive ministers, they recognize that loyalty is the most important trait for a properly balanced relationship. They watch that they do not develop an appearance of outward submission while carrying inward rebellion because loyalty must exist both privately and publicly. They always endeavor to make their pastor or spiritual leader look good.

They keep in mind that they should primarily represent the pastor to the people not the people to the pastor. It is not a compliment to them or their character if people feel they can come up and criticize the spiritual leader to them and expect them to side in with them. They will not play politics, gossip about the frailties of their leader, or sit in the seat of mockers if leadership is being verbally criticized. This projects unity to the people and also reinforces to leadership that they will never be a threat.

They recognize that any spiritual leader is human and will make mistakes, so they take them in stride without becoming bitter or disillusioned. They continue to serve God's purpose and respect the leader's office.

They become one team with one dream. They are not in competition with one another. They respect and encourage one another's expression of ministry. Their role is to provide what will complement that ministry. With the right mix of balance, they are not offended at areas that are not ones of strength for leadership but instead are willing to serve in those areas with their strengths.

They are not possessive about areas of responsibility. They graciously appreciate any decision to make some adjustments and reassignments in responsibilities. They are not surprised if given assignments that are outside their comfort zone of expertise in order to cause personal growth. They remain faithful anyway.

They get to know their leaders by studying them, watching them, and listening to them. They communicate where they are not clear on what specific things leadership had in mind for them to accomplish. With diligence, they follow through on assignments and relieving leadership from details and concerns.

They do not proceed with a Lone Ranger mentality, doing "what the Lord told me to do" with laying-on-of-hands or personal words for the flock without the prior approval of God's selected leadership for that church. They know that such actions are a reflection of a lack of maturity and absence of ministerial courtesy. In true humility and security, they welcome the "judging" of the accuracy of their words and actions as a safeguard for both themselves and for those whom they minister to (1 Cor. 14:26-33). The balanced understand that this protocol doesn't compromise their responsibility to speak for God nor does it make them mere people-pleasers.

The leaders and supportive ministers who are rightly balanced realize that there will be those whom God will bring to a local church or ministry but only for a season. If the Lord truly leads them to depart, they do so positively and peacefully in a professional fashion, giving appropriate notice. They recognize that it is wisdom to not plant negative seeds when leaving and to not burn any bridges.

Balanced believers will desire to do what is right in their submission to God and His divinely established authority in their local church. They know that God is the author of structure and delegated authority. True Sweet Po Tators will maintain a pleasant outlook and a pure heart that won't usurp church leadership. Their just right attitude in ministry is evident as they know that to God it is both what we do and with what kind of attitude we do it that matters. Their service to the fellow members at their local church is as a sweet-smelling aroma and a pleasing fragrance in the presence of the Lord.

CHAPTER 17

The Receiving Beatitudes

There are certain basic requirements necessary for a person to
have success in church leadership. Here are some unique job
descriptions for a qualified individual's resume to apply for typical
church staff leadership positions from an unknown author's rewrite
of the famous introduction to the 1950's television series, *The
Adventures of Superman:*

Senior Pastor: Able to leap tall buildings in a single bound,
more powerful than a locomotive, faster than a speeding bullet,
walks on water, and gives policy to God.

Associate Pastor: Able to leap short buildings in a single
bound, almost as powerful as a locomotive, just as fast as a speeding
bullet, walks on water (if the sea is calm), and talks with God.

Children's Church Director: Able to leap short buildings with
a running start, prefers toy trains to locomotives, faster than a
speeding B-B, walks on water (if she knows where the rocks are),
and talks with God if a special request is approved.

Music Director: Able to climb over a small building, falls off
locomotives, can fire a speeding bullet, swims well, and is occasionally addressed by God.

Youth Director: Able to run into small buildings, recognizes a
locomotive two out of three times, owns a squirt gun, knows how
to use the water fountain, and often mumble to themselves.

Church Secretary: Able to lift buildings to walk under them,
kicks locomotives off the track, catches speeding bullets in her
teeth, freezes water with a single glance, and when God speaks, she
replies, "May I ask who's calling?"

Seriously, there are different responsibilities with a church staff team, but they all require a mutual respect for each other. Whatever the position of ministry, we are to "receive one another, just as Christ also received us, to the glory of God" (Rom. 15:7). We are to reciprocate the proper receiving of one another whether we are in a church leadership position or a supportive ministerial role within that organization. Blessed are those who receive their church leader as a supportive minister and/or blessed are those who receive their supportive ministers as a church leader.

A Supportive Minister's Beatitudes of Receiving One Another

Blessed are those who faithfully serve in the role of a supportive minister. They have pledged to join with one another to connect as friends and partners in their God-ordained, glorious association with their pastor and the leadership team at their local church or ministry. They let their divine relationship unite as they minister together with their church leaders as companions in supernatural action and joined for His purpose with activities that matter to God.

Blessed are those supportive ministers who become true armor bearers who stand beside their spiritual leader to assist them, to lift them up, and to protect them. The fruit of an effective armor bearer is love, joy, peace, submission, loyalty, discipline, faithfulness, optimism, and self-control, and who avoid murmuring and complaining. Against such there is no church leader.

Blessed are those supportive ministers who are patient and tolerant to realize that God sent them to that ministry to assist, not to analyze; to support, not to critique; to serve, not to judge; and to be a body-builder, not a fault-finder. Wisdom teaches them to adapt themselves to their leader and the ministry. They recognize that God did not send them to that church or ministry to change everything to their liking but to serve their leader and minister to the people.

Blessed are those supportive ministers who become effective team players that work well with the other members of the ministry. True success is not when they look better than others but when all ministers and departments function with excellence in one accord. They have small egos and will be more embarrassed than exalted when praised publicly.

Blessed are those supportive ministers who remain teachable and willing to treat the ministries' vision with the same dedication and enthusiasm as though it were their own. They are open to helpful advice through suggestions and correction that will enhance their growth as a minister. They act on what is said, are not easily offended, and when they disagree with leadership, they do so without becoming disagreeable.

Blessed are those supportive ministers who exert energy, enthusiasm, and endurance in seeing that their leader gets a good return for the time and effort that has been invested in them. They get to know the leader's vision and goals for the ministry as well as their leader's pet peeves. They have a willingness to grow with their position and learn new skills.

Blessed are those supportive ministers who serve as a filter for leadership and for endeavoring to release them from menial responsibilities. One of the nicest things a spiritual leader can hear is a sincere inquiry of, "Is there anything else I can do for you?" They make themselves available and are a prized asset to that ministries' effectiveness.

Blessed are those supportive ministers who continually ask themselves, "If I were a church leader, what are the traits that I would want in a supporting minister?" They make note of those characteristics and endeavor to fulfill them in their own life toward the leadership God has placed over them. They trust God as He lays the foundation of character where they develop the steadiness, stability, and consistent fruit in their lives necessary to sustain long-term success in ministry.

Blessed are those supportive ministers who effectively use their time serving in their position of support whether it's on a permanent basis or in preparation for future assignments. Regardless of the final position that they are to stand in, blessed supportive ministers will treat their current assignment as though it were the most important thing they could ever do for God. In either situation, whether a supportive minister is to homestead or to help build that spiritual house before moving on, they pledge to give their fullest support and encouragement to do all that would empower one another to run the race that He has set before each of us in God's perfect timing.

Image of Christ

God, who at various times and in various ways spoke in time past to the fathers by the prophets, has in these last days spoken to us by His Son, whom He has appointed heir of all things, through whom also He made the worlds; who being the brightness of His glory and the express image of His person (Heb. 1:1-3).

Jesus was sent to this earth as the "express" image of God's person as the reflection of "the brightness of His glory." By our oneness in Him—with Christ in us and us in Christ—we are then sent to be an express image of His person as we reflect His glory to one another. By the choice of our will we purpose to become an expression of His will. We become a reflection of the brightness of His glory to one another by His indwelling love. Faith works by love as His inner love energizes our faith to receive and minister to one another (Gal. 5:6). We offer to Him our availability in exchange for His ability to receive others in His care, concern, and compassion.

The healthful spiritual life of an individual believer is dependent on the life around them. In caring only for themselves, the independent Christian suffers not only personally but their lost connection to care for their fellow brethren also causes them to have missed opportunities to receive one another as reflections of the image and likeness of His love. They deny themselves all the overflow of God's abundant life made fully possible through the help and assistance of those around them.

We are entrusted by the Lord to "warn (admonish, urge and encourage) one another every day, as long as it is called Today, that none of you may be hardened [into settled rebellion] by the deceitfulness of sin" (Heb. 3:13 Amp). The subtle deceit of isolation brings a steady decline to fallen states of sin and hardness of heart. A corporate church environment facilitates growth and maximizes spiritual development through receiving exhortations from one to another.

The expressions of Christ are found in a love that does not seek its own. Jesus' love in our hearts must overflow to those around us. We also are to put ourselves in a place to receive His love from the hearts of others. Every individual member of Christ's body is to humbly yield to be received and to receive for the well-being of all. The close communion of local church members must be demonstrated by an open reception of others that cultivates a practical care and sincere concern to express our love toward one another.

At a time when His disciples were arguing among themselves who would be the greatest in the kingdom of God, Jesus demonstrated to them that those who would receive and serve others would be greatest.

> So when He had washed their feet, taken His garments, and sat down again, He said to them, "Do you know what I have done to you? You call me Teacher and Lord, and you say well, for so I am. If I then, your Lord and Teacher, have washed your feet, you also ought to wash one another's feet... Most assuredly, I say to you, he who receives whomever I send receives Me; and

he who receives Me receives Him who sent Me" (John 13:12-14,20).

Don't miss any opportunities to receive those whom the Lord has sent into our life. The Lord demonstrated the humility of a servant as He washed the feet of His followers. As their leader, He washed their feet and commanded them to do likewise. The meekness of His character is shown in our reflection of the Lord when we faithfully serve one another. Both church leadership and their supportive ministers are to receive each other in this type of humility. The Lord is honored when we receive those He sends into our life. We honor His authority when we honor those who stand in His delegated authority. As Jesus received us as we are, we are to in turn follow His example of expression by fully receiving one another without partiality.

CHAPTER 18

The Next Generation

Our younger son is usually a slow riser in the morning. I asked Myles early one morning, "Was your sleep good?" He groggily replied, "Not yet." Another time, while I was trying to wake him, Myles sleepily said, "How did morning get here so fast?"

As children grow up so quickly, parents likewise comment, "How did their adulthood get here so fast?" We don't want to miss any opportunities to invest into the children and grandchildren of our immediate family as well as those of the younger generations in the family of God.

One time I had cancelled our usual mid-week service and encouraged our congregation to attend and support another area church meeting with a special guest minister. We knew the pastors well as they had performed our marriage. As a young couple, Deborah and I had been members at their church years before.

A fine looking young man came up to me that night and asked me if I was Fred Torneden. My first impression was good as he correctly pronounced my last name (Tore-nay-done). He remembered when I had ministered to him and the other young ones in the children's ministry there. I was encouraged even though I felt quite a bit older with a grown adult expressing his appreciation for what I had done more than twenty years earlier. I thought to myself, *How did those previous two decades get here so fast?*

This served as a reminder to me that the life of faith is like a family heirloom that must be passed on from one generation to the next. The highest of callings is to prepare the next generation for a full life of service to the Lord.

God desires every older generation to tell the next younger generation about the wonderful things He has done.

We will not hide them from their children, telling to the genera-tion to come the praises of the LORD, and His strength and His wonderful works that He has done... He commanded our fathers, that they should make them known to their children; that the generation to come might know them, the children who would be born, that they may arise and declare them to their children, that they may set their hope in God, and not forget the works of God, but keep His commandments.

Until the Lord returns, this cycle should continue from genera-tion to generation.

Generations connecting with each other are important to the Lord. The Bible uses the words "generation" and "generations" nearly 200 times. God looks at all generations as He pours out His Spirit on three generations of believers, "I will pour out of My Spirit on all flesh; Your sons and your daughters shall prophesy, Your young men shall see visions, Your old men shall dream dreams" (Acts 2:17). His Spirit is poured out on all flesh from the old to the young, including the sons and the daughters.

God looks beyond one generation to the next. Christ refer-ences a generational triad when expounding on the resurrection, "I am the God of Abraham, and God of Isaac, and the God of Jacob" (Matt. 22:32). He was God of three generations—a man, his son, and his grandson. The "I AM" is the God of multiple generations. God is not only interested in what we do for Him but also what our children and grandchildren will continue to do as they take the spiritual baton from us as effective ministers.

God used many young people throughout the Bible. Samuel was about six years old when God spoke to him concerning Eli and the judgment that was to fall for his disobedience in not disci-plining his two sons. Josiah was an eight-year-old boy king of Judah who followed several generations of wicked kings. Josiah had a tender heart for God and destroyed the idols of his day. Judgment did not come against that nation until after his reign.

Daniel and the three Hebrew children exhibited excellence in Babylon as young boys. Israel was praying for deliverance from the Philistines, and God's answer didn't come until the next generation in a young boy named Samson. The evangelist Philip had four virgin daughters who did prophesy (Acts 21:9). God used a 17-year-old boy named David to slay the giant. The Lord mightily used John, Jeremiah, Timothy, Mark, and others in the Bible who demonstrated spiritual maturity well beyond their young ages.

All people are equally valuable to Him in ministry regardless of age. We all became sons of God and heirs to the promise of eternal life in Him when we each receive Christ into our hearts through faith.

> *For you are all sons of God through faith in Christ Jesus. For as many of you as were baptized into Christ have put on Christ. There is neither Jew nor Greek, there is neither slave nor free, there is neither male nor female; for you are all one in Christ Jesus* (Gal. 3:26-28).

This wonderful salvation is for all no matter our religious background, culture, social status, gender, or age. Whether we're Jew or Gentile, poor or rich, male or female, young or old, we are all one in Christ Jesus.

His Great Commission is to the entire world, including the younger population of the world. We are to preach the gospel to every creature which includes the young. We are commissioned to go, preach, teach and make disciples of all age groups of people.

There are more people alive now than have ever lived and died. The vast majority of people alive today are children with the potential for an entire life lived for God. In the 1800s, a minister proclaimed that "ten and one-half people" had been saved in one of his meetings. Someone asked him if the one-half meant a child had been saved. He replied to the contrary that it was an adult since a grown person has already lived half their life.

We are certainly pleased when an older adult is converted late in life, but the reality is we can never make much of them. We are very glad for their eternal destination, but at seventy, what time remains for fruitful service even if they live another ten years? But when we train up a child, they may have fifty or more years of potential service for God.

Statistical research indicates that about 80 percent of the people who receive Jesus will do so before the age of fifteen. If they are not reached in their youth, then it is less likely they will respond to the Gospel. We need to reach the next generation while their hearts are still pliable and while their entire lives are ahead of them to serve God. An important responsibility of the older generation is to teach and prepare the next younger generation for their evangelistic mandate to communicate the good news to the world.

In our society, we tend to group by areas of common interest. We tend to gravitate toward those in our own generation. Our public school systems have grouped students together by age in the economical "stack 'em deep and teach 'em cheap" educational philosophy. From a young age, we tend to socialize and relate mostly with those in our own age group.

This of course has no resemblance to real life since everyday living involves interaction with all people of all age groups. What is better: for a younger person to only turn to another confused young person who is also stumbling through what they're going through or to turn to someone older who has already been there and journeyed to the other side?

The more things change the more they stay the same. Every generation thinks they are unique. They think that they bring something new to the table that previous generations haven't dealt with. Every generation deals with the same devil, the same world and the same sufferings. "Be sober, be vigilant; because your adversary the devil walks about like a roaring lion, seeking whom he may devour. Resist him, steadfast in the faith, knowing that the same sufferings are experienced by your brotherhood in the world" (1 Peter 5:8-9). It is the "same" sufferings experienced by all in the brotherhood of Christ regardless of age.

The only thing that has changed over the past few centuries has been the advancement in technology. The culture's media is exposing children to things earlier in life, but the tempter and the temptations remain the same. Yet the more technologies change the more things stay the same. Each generation's tech toys keep getting better, but no matter how much the technology in the children's toys change, the child will still play with box the toy came in.

The reality is that the younger generation will always view their parents as technophobic. Every generation will go from being on the cutting edge of the latest technology to gradually settling into their techno-grooves or tech toy ruts. The younger ones will then reap what they have sown as the day will come when their children will also view them as technophobic.

It is good for every generation to embrace their technology as long as their technology does not embrace them. The tech toys of any era can consume too much of our time so that it stunts our spiritual growth. Technological addictions of each generation can keep them from fully maturing in God's grace.

We are to build bridges that will connect generations with one another despite the obvious differences between the age groups. There are certain traits typical of older and younger generations. For example, we're probably getting older when we say things like, "I can't relate to young people these days." And we're probably younger if we say things like, "Older people can't relate to me and my generation." We're probably getting older when we are concerned about the next generation. We might be younger if we're only concerned about our generation.

We're probably getting older when we conclude that, "Youth is wasted on the young." We're probably getting older when we find ourselves saying, "When I was your age" or "Back in my day...."

We're probably getting older when it's frustrating that we're old enough to know the answers, but no one in the younger generation bothers to ask the questions. We're probably getting older when our clothing fashion statement is stuck in a certain decade, and our hair style hasn't changed in over ten years. We might be younger when we work at a retail cash register and either can't or won't count the change back.

I have taught for years at a community college, and it's certainly an ever-increasing challenge to relate to and stay engaged with 19- to 22-year-olds who are used to high levels of visual media stimulation. Our generational differences seem to become greater with each semester. I continue to age as each new wave of young twenty-something's enroll in my classes. The rewards are well worth the challenges since I feel younger in heart by working with people from a younger generation.

Our oldest son was excited in the anticipation of his upcoming birthday. Kyle asked us, "When I turn ten, will I still be young?" As one gets older, it can be a challenge to reach back to younger generations over a span of differences that seem to keep getting greater by the day. It is too easy for the older generation to stereotype the next generation as cynical, hopeless, frustrated, and unmotivated slackers. The younger ones may view the older generation as out-of-touch and not seek to learn from the life experiences of the wealth of knowledge and wisdom available of those who have preceded them.

Despite these barriers, the older generation is to erect the ceiling that the next generation stands upon. We are all the body of Christ and there ought to be a lively interaction with the older adults working with the children and youth.

Jesus gave us an excellent example to follow as He made it a priority to minister to the children of his generation. Jesus strongly rebuked his disciples for not allowing the children to be brought to Him (Mark 10:13-16). Our Lord took the time to minister to the children as well as the adults.

Jesus didn't say, "I don't have time for the children so Mary Magdalene, you set up the nursery and take care of them. Matthew, we need a special service for the youth as I'm busy with the adults. Make sure it rocks!" Jesus made it a priority to minister to all age groups.

The home and the church are the most powerful and positive influencers in the lives of children. If the parents and the church are on fire for God then they will be too. Those who are passionately in love with Jesus will demonstrate godly examples to the next generation by communicating to the youth and children that they are as much of a priority as the adults. God praised Abraham as a man who would influence "his children and household after him" in the way of the Lord (Gen. 18:19). May God commend us for influencing the younger ones in our local church.

There is a common trait that a study of church history will prove to be true of every generation of believers. There have always been those who predicted Christ's second coming in the lifetime of their generation. In every century since Jesus walked the earth, there have been those who sincerely believed that all the prophecies had been fulfilled and that they would be the generation that would usher in the return of Christ. After two millennia of this, we ought to by now have come to the realization that His soon coming is from the perspective of an eternal God who views "a thousand years as one day" (2 Pet. 3:8).

Our concept of His "soon" and "forever" may be compared to when our 6-year-old son Myles told his older brother, "If you don't stop doing that, I'm not going to talk to you forever...until next Tuesday!" What if it turns out that we too are not the final generation on the scene? We owe it to our children and the next generation to fully prepare them for the possibility of a full life of ministry.

Our life here is but a vapor to an eternal God (Jam. 4:14). Using God's ratio of a thousand years as one day, the average life span for us is about two hours from heaven's eternal perspective. If we are older, what are we doing with the vapor of our couple of hours of life to pour into the next generation? If we are younger, are we taking advantage of the opportunity to glean from the knowledge and experience of those in their second hour of life?

Lynda, our right hand support minister, volunteered when we had a need for someone to coordinate our children's ministry when we were first pioneering a new church. Before her first service with the children, God sweetly spoke to her heart, "Give it your all." We are to give our all to the Lord who gave us His all when we make ourselves available to our church's nursery, pre-school, children's or youth programs.

God takes special delight in those who will minister to the next generation of children and youth. By giving it our all, we will impart into the next generation of believers. As we look back on our life of ministry, let us not have regret and wonder, "How did my couple of hours of life get here so fast?" We can each leave a spiritual legacy of ministry planted into the next generation for a harvest that will continue well after our life race here is run.

CHAPTER 19

Rest in Work

The world has made many humorous observations concerning the subject of work:

Most people work just hard enough not to get fired and get paid just enough money not to quit.

The world is full of willing people; some willing to work, the rest willing to let them.

Hard work never killed anybody, but why take a chance?

Back in high school, I would take summer employment opportunities with local farmers to pick up bales of hay. It was hard and hot work to earn the minimum wage of two dollars an hour. It was a popular thing to jokingly ask each other, "Are you working hard or hardly working?"

I recently noticed a bumper sticker that said, "Look busy. He's coming soon." When Jesus returns will the Lord find His church just looking busy or actually working? Will we each be found hardly working or working hard in our ministry of expression to one another? And will our attitudes and ministry efforts be a reflection that is pleasing in His sight?

Work is part of God's created order for humanity. In the beginning, God commanded Adam and Eve to "tend and keep" the Garden of Eden (Gen. 2:15). Work is normal and to be expected. Paul said, "If anyone will not work, neither shall he eat" and to "work in quietness" to eat our own bread (2 Thess. 3:10-12).

Everything that we bring to work (our skills, intelligence, experience, and reputation) is a gift from God that He allows us to use. God's original intention for work was to bless us. He blesses each one by "all the work of your hands" (Deut. 16:15).

God seems to relate best to those who know how to work. He calls those that were first faithful in their previous work. When Elijah called Elisha to be his successor, he was found to be busy doing his family business in the field with twelve yoke of oxen. When Samuel came to anoint David as king, he was tending his father's herds of sheep as Jesse's youngest son. Paul was one of the most zealous religious men of his day at the time of his Damascus road experience. Even in the demands of apostolic ministry, Paul still was willing to maintain a business as a tent maker by trade (Acts 18:3). God calls those who are first productive and willing to work hard.

Paul used the terms workers and laborers in the context of our ministry with God. "We, then, as workers together with Him also plead with you not to receive the grace of God in vain" (2 Cor. 6:1). "For we are labourers together with God" (1 Cor. 3:9 KJV). We are all expected to be workers and laborers together with God and one another.

Ministry is considered work. God gave the gift of a pastor "for the equipping of the saints for the work of ministry" (Eph. 4:11,12). There is a reason it is called the "work" of ministry. Our expressions of His love toward one another are an important aspect of our call to the work of our individual ministry.

Work is a physical or mental effort or activity directed toward the production or accomplishment of something. The work in the expression of our personal ministry is to accomplish the edification of the body of Christ. By our connection with a local church, we give our supply and do our share of the work of the ministry.

Real ministry is more than what we observe with our pastor in the pulpit on Sunday mornings. Behind the scenes, there is so much more work that can become quite menial and labor intensive. This is where every joint finds their ministry as productive members who do their share along with the whole body of believers united in that corporate ministries' activity.

We need to make every reasonable effort to participate fully in local church services. To just show up to only attend church when it's most convenient leads to it becoming ever less and less convenient. Then more compromises and more excuses will fuel a continued cycle of lack of attendance and commitment to the work of our ministry to one another. Most people only need to give up some time spent with television programs to have adequate time for church and other life priorities.

Let's give the work of the church the priority it deserves. If we are scheduled as an usher or children's minister, then we need to be fully prepared to give it our very best. The most effective helps volunteers and supportive ministers are those who by prayerful spiritual preparation are in the zone for their ministerial position by the time they arrive at church.

We shouldn't be like a short-order cook who always whips up something real fast. Instead let's be a gourmet chef, who has spent time with the Holy Spirit to plan and prepare an inspired feast fresh from heaven. We shouldn't fall into a mindset of wondering if we are scheduled to work in our department as we are driving to church. We can be like the true remnant army who has spent time in spiritual preparation in His boot camp rather than a civilian who just haphazardly wings it.

Balance Needed

There is however an important balance to life and ministry. As there are issues with under-working, there are also problems to over-working. Work without becoming a workaholic. The demands of over-work cause one to neglect their health, their family and the time they need to spend with God in prayer or rejuvenating through recreation and rest. Every day we make crucial decisions about how to spend our time and energy to keep the right priorities in mind. These priorities are best achieved when we fit work into our life rather than trying to build our life around work.

There are those people who burn out from being over-committed with the work of ministry. After years of engagement, they completely drop out from any active commitment. Almost overnight, they went from speeding to park. I shake my head at how once faithful saints who were pillars in their local church go from maximized service to no service at all.

There certainly will be times when church leadership does take advantage of willing volunteers. There are pastors who take on a task-oriented management philosophy and overwork the twenty percent who try to do eighty percent of the work. People need to learn that "no" can be an anointed word. I'm not implying we should say no to commitment but rather we need to say no to over-commitment. Instead of completely dropping out of service, let's cut back to a sensible service level. We shouldn't let it get to the breaking point where we suddenly quit all together. The answer is not to drop out and quit but to pace our race in personal ministry.

The Christian life is compared to a race. To begin profits nothing unless we run to the finish line. There is the old cliché, "Quitters never win and winners never quit." As a former successful distance runner, I know the importance of pacing in a race. A marathon is a long-endurance event not a sprint. There are kickers who either start out too fast or save too much back for the sprint at the finish. Anyone can go out hard while they are relatively fresh.

One of my college coaches told us not to lead in the beginning stages of the race. We were instructed to follow, conserve our energy in the pack, and make our move later in the race when the early leaders were most tired. It is what a runner does in the middle and later stages of the race that will determine if they race to their potential anyway. When we go out too hard too early, we are writing checks with our mind that our body won't be able to cash late in the race. When we don't pace our race, we'll lack the stamina to push through the tougher stages of the run. Likewise, we need to pace ourselves in life and ministry. Be a steady Freddie or a stable Mable with an even-paced approach in our spiritual race here on earth.

The correct response when we are sidelined and burned out from overwork is to get back in the race and do the work of ministry at a sensible pace. We are to run our race like a steady marathoner by being committed without becoming over-committed. Ephesians 4:16 admonishes us concerning "the whole body" by what "every joint supplies," and "every part does its share." It doesn't say anything about any joints over-supplying or any part doing more than its share.

Church ought to be a place where the committed do not over-commit. Churches attract idealists who are highly conscientious persons. They become over-committed by over-identifying themselves with their positions, causing them to burnout. Burnout can become a psychological wound that lasts long after the original fatigue since people who have experienced it suffer from a false sense of guilt for not living up to their own expectations. Church ought to be a place where we can find fulfillment as balanced, active participants.

God's Plan

We are to find out what God specifically wants us to do in the work of ministry. Many church committees make their plans and then ask God to bless those plans. If they find out what God's plans are then they can be confident that it is already blessed. Let God plan our work, then we work that plan. There is a grace that comes with doing what God has told us to do. There is a rest in the Lord while we are doing what we are asked to do. In fact, He wants us to have a rest in our work. Rest in work may seem like an oxymoron, but we can learn how to do it. He makes it very clear how to get His rest.

> *Come to Me, all you who labor and are heavy laden, and I will give you rest. Take My yoke upon you and learn from Me, for I am gentle and lowly in heart, and you will find rest for your souls. For My yoke is easy and My burden is light* (Matt. 11:28-30).

A yoke speaks of work with the Lord, and His work yoke is easy. We are to supply our load, but as we learn from Him, it will be a light load. When we work in Him, with Him, and by Him, we find His rest in the midst of our work in the ministry. There is nothing more fulfilling than to be in the center of His will and to be used by the Lord to help others, to lead someone to Christ, or give another person a word of encouragement that changes their life.

I have learned about work and rest from my experiences as a former marathon distance runner. There are times to train hard. There are also equally important times to rest and recover from the intermittent times of hard work. An experienced athlete knows to train and not strain. There is an overload principle in progression of workouts where over-training can occur in athletics.

My primary job with coaching inexperienced athletes was to motivate them to train hard enough. Then my primary task for coaching the experienced athlete was to watch that their high motivation didn't cause them to train too hard. There is a proper balance with hard training mixed with proper recovery.

The disciples had just returned exhausted from when the Lord had sent them out for ministry. "And He said to them, 'Come aside by yourselves to a deserted place and rest a while.' For there were many coming and going, and they did not even have time to eat. So they departed to a deserted place in the boat by themselves" (Mark 6:30-32). We have this example in scripture to reveal our need for times of rest to refresh and let our batteries recharge.

We need private time to cut loose, goof off, and leisurely play. These are times to be spent by ourselves, alone with God, or for quality time with those close to us. These are times to relax, go out to eat, or even to do a few impractical things. Life can't be about staying on a rigid schedule, sticking to an inflexible plan, or eating vegetables all the time.

It is the dream to have the work of the ministry become fun and the interpersonal relationships enjoyable. God grants us the freedom and permission to spontaneously have fun and laugh. In the beginning, even God Himself rested after His six days of work (Gen. 2:2-3).

There is a time for work and a time for rest. We can learn from Him about how to work restfully in Him and truly rest when it's time to rest. My wife, Deborah, knows well that I both know how to work and to rest efficiently. I can go from a total work mode to a total rest mode in a moment's time. I most enjoy the time of the day when I fully repose, quietly wait on Him, and rest in the Lord spiritually, mentally, emotionally, and physically.

The work of the ministry can become so busy that we no longer make time to passionately pursue our intimate love for Him within our prayer closets. We will be able to keep on in service if we maintain quality fellowship time with our Lord and Spirit of God. We can stay strong by pursuing and maintaining times of refreshing by waiting on Him, praying in seclusion, and feeding on His Word.

There are two alarming statistics true of pastors and those in paid ministerial positions. First, there are nearly 1,500 people who quit the pulpit ministry monthly; and second, because of the time demands of ministry, the majority of pastors pray less than five minutes a day. These two facts are probably related to one another. Less would dropout and quit if they made more time to rest in the Lord's presence with regular times of prayer.

The ministry is work, but that work becomes a rest when we

do it all *with* Him and *for* Him. "And whatever you do, do it heartily, as to the Lord and not to men, knowing that from the Lord you will receive the reward of the inheritance; for you serve the Lord Christ" (Col. 3:23-24). Ministry is for Him and not for someone else.

By keeping our eyes on Him, we won't quit when we feel under appreciated by man. By glorifying Him, we won't be concerned whether we receive any glory from the people we serve. By dedicating all we do to Him, we won't be tempted to give up when the going gets tough. We will stick it out no matter what our circumstance when we are doing our work to Him and not to men. We might be serving God's people, but that service is ultimately to God. We will enter His rest with the right attitude and motivation in our work of ministry.

There is a rest intended for God's people. We are instructed to "be diligent to enter that rest" (Heb. 4:9-11). There is a rest found in Him when we keep in mind that "God is not unjust to forget your work and labor of love which you have shown toward His name, in that you have ministered to the saints, and do minister" (Heb. 6:10). As we take on His easy yoke of work, we find the proper rhythms of life that require a difficult balancing act. We will find His load to be light with a healthy balance between work and play. There is restfulness for our soul with the right ebb and flow to everyday life between work and rest, the spectacular and the mundane, the extraordinary and ordinary, the supernatural and the natural.

CHAPTER 20

Great Zeal

I remember standing on the starting line to compete in the 1984 Houston Marathon on a cold January morning. It was an Olympic year, and the competitive quality of the international field of race entrants was impressive. By local Texas standards, it was an absolutely freezing day. To me, it was nice and toasty as I had already endured a colder than normal winter up north in Kansas in preparation for this race. While I was acclimated to the cold, many of the runners from warmer weather climates faltered due to the frigid temperatures.

I made one mistake of wearing new racing flats that my shoe sponsors had provided for me the day before the race. The shoes turned out to be too small in the toe box. My shoes and socks were blood soaked by the end of the race from multiple blisters on my toes and the tops of my feet. My feet were sore for several days, and I later lost a couple of toenails.

Other than the annoyance of the pain from the blisters, the pace in the front pack had seemed relatively comfortable until I hit a bad patch with five miles to go. I started to see spots as when one is about to faint. Quitting was not an option. I did what one of my college coaches taught me and sped up the pace to change my rhythm until the discomfort subsided.

It's been said that finishing a 26.2 mile marathon is the most painful thing one can voluntarily put themselves through, second only to giving birth to a child. It is understandable why God had women have the babies since the majority of men could never have handled the labor pains.

To me, it was worth the momentary suffering I endured when I placed fifth in that marathon and improved my previous best time by more than two minutes. It takes great zeal to maintain our spiritual pace when life's blisters and adverse weather conditions challenge our motivation to get to the finish line.

"These hard times are small potatoes compared to the coming good times, the lavish celebration prepared for us. There's far more here than meets the eye. The things we see now are here today, gone tomorrow. But the things we can't see now will last forever" (2 Cor. 4:17-18 Message). Don't let the "small potatoes" of these hard times take us out of reaching the glory of our finish line that will last forever.

I would tell myself as an athlete and my athletes as a coach, "When the going gets tough, the tough get going." Like a coach in the pulpit, I've told our congregation, "When the going gets tough, those through Christ get going." We can do all things through Christ who strengthens us (Phil. 4:13).

The mindset of marathoners is quite unique in dealing with the miles and miles of trials of long distance running. They learn to sustain their pace through rough patches with the attitude that says that pain is just weakness leaving the body. They try to convince themselves that, "What doesn't kill you will make you stronger" and "What doesn't break you will make you." The great Kenyan distance runners have an inspiring motto, "Run to the death then sprint." We can reflect the Lord's great zeal and fervency for empowerment and see our race through all the way to our finish line victoriously in Him.

In his epistles to the churches, Paul made several references to disciplined running and racing. He wrote,

> *Do you not know that those who run in a race all run, but one receives the prize? Run in such a way that you may obtain it. And everyone who competes for the prize is temperate in all things. Now they do it to obtain a perishable crown, but we for*

an imperishable crown. Therefore I run thus: not with uncertainty. Thus I fight: not as one who beats the air. But I discipline my body and bring it into subjection, lest, when I have preached to others, I myself should become disqualified (1 Cor. 9:24-27).

Various translations use many vivid descriptions to his statement, "I discipline my body and bring it unto subjection." The word "discipline" is also rendered drive, punish, buffet, bruise, pommel, and give blows to the body. The *New International Version* says, "I beat my body and make it my slave." Through my previous athletic experiences, I can certainly relate to the difficulties of running through pain barriers during the course of a long distance race.

At the end of his life, Paul declared to Timothy, "I have fought the good fight, I have finished the race, I have kept the faith" (2 Tim. 4:7). Paul had written these statements in this letter just days before he was sentenced to die. Historical traditions state that he was beheaded by the Roman Emperor Nero. Paul acknowledged, "For I am already being poured out as a drink offering, and the time of my departure is at hand" (2 Tim. 4:6). Despite all his many difficulties, Paul maintained the zeal to fight the good fight and finish his race with joy while keeping the faith. He said,

But none of these things move me; nor do I count my life dear to myself, so that I may finish my race with joy, and the ministry which I received from the Lord Jesus, to testify to the gospel of the grace of God (Acts 20:24).

I have learned much about how to deal with life from having been a no-nonsense distance runner and coach. I maintained that the harder one trained, the faster they would race. It challenged my coaching patience when young athletes would brag to one another about how good they were. I just laughed to myself when they would boast about how fast they were going to race when they weren't paying the price in their training to get there.

Talk is cheap. I appreciated the soft-spoken athletes who would simply let their walking do their talking. They didn't need to convince others or themselves that they were good. They simply let their actions speak for them.

I grew up in the country where I observed plenty of farm dogs. The dogs who barked the most were usually the ones who were the most afraid. I learned to watch out though for the quiet dogs who would just growl with that look in their eyes. I preferred to coach the athletes who are that way. They are what I called "silent assassins." They knew they were good and didn't need to verbalize it. They would simply walk the talk.

Coaches like to tell their athletes, "It's not the size of the dog in the fight. It's the size of the fight in the dog." With us, it's not the size of the Christian in the Lord. It's the size of the Lord in the Christian. Know who we are in Christ, but more importantly, know who Christ is in us.

All of us have seen the Beware of Dog signs used on property fences. It's comical to me when that dog turns out to be a smallish (and perhaps wimpy) toy dog. One day when I was out running, I spotted a fence sign that got my attention, "Warning—Bad Dog!" Needless to say, I gave that yard plenty of clearance.

We need to be what I like to call "a dangerous dawg" who is a radically, sold out Christian disciple. Even if we are a smallish, toy-like dog in our own outward ability, we can live large and in charge by His inward ability. Let's have a reputation in hell as a zealous "bad dog" Christian who knows their authority and place in Jesus Christ.

We are to run with endurance and patience the race that God has set before each of us.

> *Therefore we also, since we are surrounded by so great a cloud of witnesses, let us lay aside every weight, and the sin which so easily ensnares us, and let us run with endurance the race that is set before us, looking unto Jesus, the author and finisher of our*

154

faith, who for the joy that was set before Him endured the cross, despising the shame, and has sat down at the right hand of the throne of God. For consider Him who endured such hostility from sinners against Himself, lest you become weary and discouraged in your souls (Heb. 12:1-3).

Weariness and discouragement can come when we stop looking unto Jesus and considering Him. By keeping our eyes on Him, glorifying Him, and dedicating all we do to Him, we won't be tempted to give up when the going gets tough. Our zeal won't wane, and we will not quit when we feel under appreciated by man.

He is the finisher of our faith who will see us through to our spiritual finish line. The joy that was set before Him is what enabled Him to endure the sufferings and the shame of the cross. He endured the hostility from sinners as He considered the will of the Father who sent Him.

We will stay zealous in ministry as we continue to consider the rich rewards of heaven's inheritance that comes from God not man. Our primary motivation is to be an expression and a reflection of Him to others out of our love for Him and His eternal reward, not for any earthly payment or benefits.

For example, the majority of helps ministry within a local church is done without financial compensation. Most of our expressed ministry to one another is provided in the local church as volunteer help. The Lord once told me as a pastor of a local church that "The best pay comes from the volunteer positions in the church when done with the right heart."

Before I became a pastor, a visiting minister came to the church in which I was serving. I was frazzled that weekend with coordinating the ushers and other behind-the-scenes activities in preparation for the church services. This guest minister privately pulled me aside to personally encourage me at a time when I was feeling weary, over-worked, and under-appreciated. He told me, "I know, and more importantly, God knows all that you are doing here for Him."

We need to be assured that God fully knows our level of faithfulness and the attitude by which we do the tasks that reflect Jesus to one another. Let's always keep in mind that payday from the Lord is coming. His heavenly check for faithfulness is in the mail, scheduled to arrive in due season. Rewards are waiting for us, not only in this life, but more importantly in heaven, for our faithfulness to serve Him with zeal here on earth.

Our zeal to maintain faithfulness in our ministry to others is to ever consider the eternal reward that will come when we stand before the King. Our inheritance of reward will not be fully given today or at the end of the week or month by man here in this life. Our payday is coming, though, for our labor in the Lord and for the righteous Judge. Giving provides the greatest fulfillment that we can ever know. Look to and consider the One who will not forget our work and labor of love as we continue to minister to His saints.

Whatever you do, do it heartily, as to the Lord and not to men, knowing that from the Lord you will receive the reward of the inheritance, for you serve the Lord Christ (Col. 3:23-24).

God looks at the attitude of the heart as to whether our service to Him was done heartily or not. We are to guard the attitude of our hearts so that we perform our expression to others with gladness and joy. Our labor toward one another is not in vain when done "heartily as to the Lord." We make ourselves available to men but do so as unto the Lord. Whether a ministry position is paid or not, it should be done primarily for heaven's reward not for earthly payment or recognition.

No person can take us out of our ministry to one another by offense and hurt if we continually do it "heartily, as to the Lord and not men." Our eyes are on Him as we know where our reward of inheritance comes from. We are serving the Lord and not men. The greatest reward comes from heaven anyway.

As we continue to look to the Lord in whatever we do, we will stay committed, enthusiastic, motivated, faithful, and reliable. Looking for our reward from men can drain us of our energy. Men can and will disappoint us and sideline us from effectively running our spiritual race of personal ministerial expression. Any ministry effort can become short-circuited to Him, to the world, and to His church, if not done heartily as to God. Look unto Him and His eternal retirement plan for our reward of the inheritance.

Paul commended Epaphras for his great zeal. "Epaphras, who is one of you, a bondservant of Christ, greets you, always laboring fervently for you in prayer that you may stand perfect and complete in all the will of God. For I bear witness that he has a great zeal" (Col. 4:12-13). His example and zeal serves to motivate us to likewise be "always laboring fervently." The challenge is to maintain great zeal through to our finish line. It takes much zeal and discipline to complete the training and put forth the effort to finish well in a marathon race.

We are to "Be kindly affectionate to one another with brotherly love, in honor giving preference to one another; not lagging in diligence, fervent in spirit, serving the Lord" (Rom. 12:10-11). There are other translations for "fervent in spirit" in Romans 12:11: "Be glowing in spirit." "Have your spirits aglow." "On fire with the Spirit." "Be aglow with the Spirit." "Maintain the spiritual glow." "Be aglow and burning with the spirit" (Amp). The fervency of our spirits is to be white hot in our diligence and zeal to serve the Lord and the body of Christ.

Paul told Timothy to stir up the gift of God within him. "Therefore I remind you to stir up the gift of God which is in you " (2 Tim. 1:6). The Amplified translation says to "stir up—rekindle the embers, fan the flame, and keep burning." Let's not fall into the trap of waiting to be stirred up by the Spirit when God is waiting for us to first stir up the One Who was sent to assist us. His zeal is within us by His Spirit. We need to tap into His fervency already resident within our spirit by the Spirit of God. In other words, we need to stir up His great zeal already in us.

God's Spirit within us is a Spirit of power and might, not weakness and inertia. His life within is a moving force, always active and flowing. As born-again believers, the life of God is available to draw upon at all times. God works through us, but He doesn't do everything for us. God created us to be active and energetic. God desires to move through us as the person He created us to be—an active, glowing, and moving force for the kingdom of God. God has a miracle supply within us all if we make the choice to activate Him by stirring up the gift of His Spirit.

He gives us the victory as we remain steadfast in ministry.

But thanks be to God, who gives us the victory through our Lord Jesus Christ. Therefore, my beloved brethren, be steadfast, immovable, always abounding in the work of the Lord, knowing that your labor is not in vain in the Lord" (1 Cor. 15:57-58).

Our zeal to serve the Lord by our expressions that minister to one another is part of the race that He has set before each of us. As we keep our eyes on the goal, we won't quit our race no matter how difficult it may get. It's been said, "If you're going through hell, keep going." No matter what we may be going through we can keep going with great zeal as we remain focused on the One who is waiting for us at the finish line. Then we will stay committed, enthusiastic, motivated, and faithful in our labor of ministry.

May we all be able to declare at the end of our life, "I have fought the good fight, I have finished the race, I have kept the faith." We will have know the thrill of victory as we finish our race of ministry joyfully to Him and to His church and accomplish the perfect will of God through our Lord Jesus Christ.

About the Author

Author Fred Torneden shares biblical insights from his personal experiences as a husband, father, pastor, college teacher, world class marathoner, and national Coach of the Year. Fred is a minister dedicated to the lost as he has partnered and traveled with seasoned evangelists to Asia, Africa and the Middle East. As a gifted guest teacher, Fred encourages congregations to find their place of Christian expression in the local church and receive the gift of a pastor.

Contact Information:
Rivers of Glory Ministries/
Go Evangelism International
PO Box 121
Andover, Kansas 67002

fredtorneden.org